Environmental Responsibility

An agenda for

further and higher education

Report of a Committee on Environmental Education
in Further and Higher Education, appointed by the
Department for Education and the Welsh Office

Chairman:

Peter Toyne

London: HMSO

Department for Education
Sanctuary Buildings
Great Smith Street
London SW1P 3BT

Tel. 071-925 5000

Welsh Office
Training, Enterprise and Education Department
4th Floor
Companies House
Crown Way
Cardiff CF4 3UT

Tel. 0222 388588

ISBN 0 11 270820 X

RECYCLED PAPER

Edited by DFE Information Branch

Contents

Preface

Bottle banks at local supermarkets and car parks; recycling centres in leafy suburbs; 'clean up' campaigns in urban wastelands; demonstrations in local beauty spots; popular support for all kinds of environmental 'causes'; colour supplements issuing warnings of imminent ecological disaster – the litany of lobbying is such that it would be tempting to conclude that environmental awareness and responsibility are firmly on the nation's agenda.

It was against this background of allegedly heightened public awareness and concern that we were asked to examine the present state of environmental education in further and higher education (FHE) in England and Wales, and make an assessment of what needs to be done, now, to provide the workforce with the knowledge, skills and awareness which it will need to assume greater environmental responsibility.

Our conclusion is simple. There is yet much to be done, it needs doing urgently and it will require concerted effort. It is a common task which needs to be taken up by all who are involved in the provision of FHE.

Being over-prescriptive in our recommendations would, however, be counterproductive. Rather, what is needed is that everyone (the providers as well as the clients in FHE) assume 'ownership' of the common task. That is why our principal recommendation is that every FHE institution should *itself* adopt an appropriately time-tabled strategy for the development of environmental education. And that strategy will have no credibility unless the institution proclaiming it adopts and implements a wider strategy for the improvement of all aspects of its environmental performance. Institutions simply must practise what they teach!

In their pursuit of this task, the institutions will need the support and collaboration of many agencies, including Government; the Further and Higher Education Funding Councils; the many professional, examining, validating and accrediting bodies who control or influence FHE curricula; and last but by no means least employers. We recognise that the task is immense – and certainly far greater than might be imagined from a recitation of the litany identified above. There is a long way to go in creating environmental education that will produce rounded citizens, acceptable employees and sensitive policy-formulators and managers fine-tuned to the environmental revolution that has already begun. But that is all the more reason to be making an urgent start on the common task.

Our thanks are due to all those who have contributed, in whatever way, to our work as a Committee. Organisations and individuals who provided information and advice, orally or in writing, are listed in Annexes B and C. We are also grateful for the help we have received from various Government Departments, including the Employment Department and the Department of the Environment; and in particular for the sterling work of our DFE Secretariat, who have made a major contribution to the work of the Committee and have been largely responsible for the preparation of our Report.

Those who provided us with information and advice (in whatever form) are listed — with apologies for any inadvertent omissions — in Annex C. In thanking them all, we would like to mention in particular the help we received from Ms Shirley Ali Khan, who kindly shared with us much useful information arising from her recent work on behalf of the Committee of Directors of Polytechnics, the Council for Environmental Education and the Further Education Unit (FEU).

Peter Toyne
Chairman
Committee on Environmental Education
January 1993

Summary of main findings

The environmental agenda

Greater

Our understanding of what it means to be 'environmentally responsible' has been transformed in recent years. Science has highlighted the complexity of the environmental systems which support life on earth, and the extent to which their delicate balance is being put at risk by apparently innocuous human activity. Global warming, ozone depletion and the maintenance of biodiversity are among the major issues on the contemporary 'environmental agenda'.

An adequate response to this agenda will call for a greatly heightened sense of 'environmental responsibility', extending far beyond industries traditionally seen as 'dirty'. All forms of economic activity have a potential impact on the environment, in terms of the resources they use and the way they use them. Organisations which make limited use of natural resources themselves may greatly influence the use of resources by others. All sectors of the economy must seek to improve their 'environmental performance', and will face increasing legislative and other pressure to do so.

The workforce's need for greater environmental understanding

Everybody has some scope for doing his or her job in a more environmentally responsible way, and needs to understand the importance of this. A basic level of environmental awareness is therefore needed across the workforce as a whole. But many individuals will need more than this, either because they have been given specific environmental responsibilities within their organisations, or simply because their organisation's environmental impact is heavily dependent on the way they carry out their day-to-day tasks, and on the decisions – technical, managerial, commercial – which they have to take.

How FHE should respond to the needs of the workforce

Developing these levels of environmental knowledge, skills and understanding is a major task which must involve many other parties besides FHE. But FHE has an indispensable role to play by providing:

- Specialist courses leading to specifically environmental qualifications.

- 'Updating' courses for those already in the workforce.

- Environmental education for all students, whatever their specialist subjects of study.

The respective roles of these three 'strands' are likely to shift. Some current 'updating' needs relate to knowledge which future members of the workforce will have acquired through their initial education in schools and FHE. Labour market demand for holders of specialist 'environmental qualifications' has in general been modest but may increase, at least for some types of qualification. But there will be an important ongoing role for all three strands.

In relation to each strand, the Committee's main findings are:

'Specialist' environmental courses leading to qualifications

- Current 'specialist' provision ranges widely and includes courses (at all levels from FE to postgraduate HE) which are geared more or less closely to the requirements of particular environmental occupations, as well as courses (very largely at first degree level) with broader educational objectives.

- Course titles are often opaque and unhelpful to employers.

- *Student* demand is generally buoyant. Relative to *employer* demand, however, clear evidence of current shortfalls in provision is confined to one or two subjects.

- Some increase in demand is likely for persons with specialist qualifications at postgraduate and sub-degree level: and also, quite possibly, for holders of vocationally focussed first degrees in such subjects as Environmental Technology.

- FHE is likely to be able to meet this increase in demand, but the situation should be monitored.

- Broadly based degree courses in Environmental Science and Environmental Studies have a potentially important part to play in the development of an environmentally responsible workforce. In many cases, however, there is need for a reappraisal of course content and objectives in the light of the employment opportunities actually available to graduates. There is also a need to ensure that graduates' capabilities are more widely understood by employers, especially in industry.

- Some existing syllabuses, at least in FE, will need to be significantly modified in response to the introduction of National Vocational Qualifications (NVQs).

- More flexible methods of course-delivery are needed, particularly in the case of postgraduate courses; flexibility will in any case be at a premium where NVQs are involved.

Keeping the workforce up to date

- The workforce's need for environment-related 'updating' is widely recognised in principle by major employers, but the progress they have so far made in identifying their detailed requirements is more variable.

- Among small and medium-sized enterprises, the general level of awareness is likely to be very much lower.

- A substantial increase in demand for updating can be expected as employers appreciate their environmental training needs more clearly.

- FHE will face strong competition from other training providers for a share in this expanding market, but should still be capable of raising its – currently very variable – levels of activity considerably.

- Not all FHE institutions are equally well-placed to provide environment-related updating, but each institution should make a serious assessment of its potential in this field.

- Relevant expertise and facilities will be widely dispersed across an institution's departments and faculties. To develop a substantial programme, mechanisms must be in place to mobilise and co-ordinate these resources. Staff development will also be required.

- A considerable improvement in communication between FHE and employers is needed.

Environmental education for the student body at large ('Cross-Curricular Greening')

- FHE has an important part to play in developing the environmental understanding of students whose courses are not specifically 'environmental' in focus.

- Such 'cross-curricular greening' may be concerned with work-related needs, or more broadly with the students' needs as citizens. In practice, much provision may address both sets of needs concurrently.

- Although many employers see a need for 'greening', it has not so far received the attention it deserves either from FHE institutions or from national examining, validating and accrediting bodies.

- 'Greening' cannot be expected to develop at the same pace, or according to the same priorities, in every institution. But every institution should be setting the process in hand.

- Environmental education for 'non-specialist' students may be delivered either through self-contained modules, or by developing environmental themes which arise naturally from the students' main subjects of study.

- In practice a combination of these strategies is likely to be needed, although the range of academic subjects providing scope for the integration of environmental issues is much wider than might be supposed.

- The development of a common level of environmental understanding across the whole of an institution's student body is a difficult objective to achieve in the short term, but experiments towards this end should be encouraged.

The way forward

Action will be needed locally and nationally to promote the further development of environmental education within FHE. In particular:

- Every FHE institution should adopt and implement an appropriately timetabled and prioritised strategy for the development of environmental education, and also a wider strategy for the improvement of all aspects of its environmental performance as an institution. These strategies should be based on full consultation within the institution, to ensure the widest possible commitment to their effective implementation.

- Particularly, though not only in relation to updating, institutions should seek to improve their dialogue with employers (who should be willing to reciprocate).

- Support should be provided for institutions through a centrally funded curriculum development programme and other action to disseminate good practice.

- The Further and Higher Education Funding Councils should take steps to encourage and reward the adoption of sound environmental practice in the institutions which they fund.

- Examining, validating, accrediting and professional bodies should facilitate – and where appropriate require – the inclusion of relevant environmental issues in courses for which they control or influence the curricula.

- Government should seek ways and means of encouraging closer dialogue between FHE and employers.

- Further research may be needed into the current and likely future needs of employers, particularly small and medium enterprises.

Specific recommendations

General

After consultation with its staff and students, every FHE institution should formally adopt and publicise, by the beginning of the academic year 1994/95, a comprehensive environmental policy statement, together with an action plan for its implementation (paragraph 7.6).

The Further and Higher Education Funding Councils should take appropriate action to encourage and reward the adoption of sound environmental practice in the institutions which they fund (paragraph 7.8).

Each institution, pursuant to its overall environmental policy, should adopt a policy for the development of environmental education (paragraph 5.16, 6.13, 7.10).

Funds should be provided for a national programme to support the development of environmental education within FHE through the identification and dissemination of good practice, the production and dissemination of teaching and learning materials, and the establishment of a database of materials already available (paragraph 7.26).

The Department for Education, the Welsh Office and the Department of the Environment should investigate the feasibility of establishing a national awards scheme to recognise outstanding progress by individual institutions in the development of environmental education, and in the improvement of their overall environmental performance as institutions (paragraph 7.28).

Insofar as future funding arrangements for FHE involve earmarked provision for staff development in particular subject areas, serious consideration should be given by the Further and Higher Education Funding Councils to the claims of environmental education (paragraph 7.20).

The Department for Education and the Welsh Office should commission, not later than the academic year 1995/96, a national appraisal of the progress which FHE has made in the development of environmental education against the background of the Committee's Report; and should consider the need for further action at national level in the light of this appraisal (paragraph 8.4).

Specialist environmental course provision

The need for research to establish firmer evidence of likely trends in employer demand for persons holding specialist environmental qualifications should be further considered by the Employment Department in consultation with the Department for Education, the Welsh Office, the Department of the Environment and the Training and Enterprise Councils (paragraph 4.5).

First degree courses

All higher education institutions providing first degree courses in Environmental Science or Environmental Studies should undertake a searching review of their aims and curricula, in the light of their recent graduates' employment destinations (paragraph 4.21).

Prospectuses and other information for prospective students should be kept under constant review, with particular reference to what is said or implied about career outlets (paragraph 4.29).

Institutions which do not at present offer work experience placements for their students should seriously consider doing so; where placements are already offered, institutions should explore the scope for increasing their variety. Employers should make every effort to collaborate with institutions in this (paragraph 4.24).

The scope for achieving greater consistency in the use of 'environmental' course-titles should be considered by the Committee of Heads of Environmental Sciences, in consultation with the Institution of Environmental Sciences and other relevant interested bodies (paragraph 4.27).

The feasibility of establishing a 'core curriculum' for first degree courses in Environmental Science and Environmental Studies should be examined by the Committee of Heads of Environmental Sciences (paragraph 4.15).

Taught postgraduate courses

The Employment Department, in consultation with the Department for Education, the Welsh Office and the Department of the Environment, should monitor trends in employer demand for persons with postgraduate environmental qualifications, and also keep the development of provision under careful surveillance, to ensure that any shortages or bottlenecks are speedily identified (paragraph 4.41).

Institutions currently offering – or planning to offer – taught postgraduate courses in environmental subjects should take all practicable steps to improve the flexibility of their delivery, for example through modularisation and distance learning (paragraph 4.44).

Updating

In the context of their overall environmental strategies, all FHE institutions should seriously consider the scope for extending their involvement in environment-related updating (paragraph 5.16).

Environmental updating should be given priority – both by institutions and by the Further and Higher Education Funding Councils – in the allocation of any funds which may be available to support the development of updating in general (paragraph 5.20).

To ensure that environment-related updating needs are more clearly articulated for the guidance of providers, the Department for Education, the Welsh Office, the Employment Department, the Department of Trade and Industry and the Department of the Environment should urgently investigate ways and means of encouraging better communication between FHE and employers, building on networks and mechanisms which already exist (paragraph 5.31).

The Employment Department and the Welsh Office should encourage Training and Enterprise Councils to give closer attention to the need for greater day-to-day environmental responsibility in industry, and the training requirements arising from this (paragraph 5.30).

The Government should consider the case for research into the particular training needs of small and medium-sized enterprises (paragraph 5.32).

Institutions involved in environment-related updating should explore with their industrial and other clients the scope for staff secondments (in both directions), to promote mutual understanding and improve the quality and relevance of their provision (paragraph 5.28).

The Department for Education, in consultation with the Welsh Office, should investigate the feasibility of developing a national directory of environment-related updating provision and other environmental services provided by FHE (paragraph 5.23), and should also consider how the dissemination of successful environment-related updating practice might best be achieved (paragraph 5.24).

Cross-curricular greening

Each institution's policy for environmental education should include, in particular, a strategy for the promotion of environmental education across the curriculum, together with an action plan for its implementation (paragraph 6.13).

All parties concerned with the future development of General National Vocational Qualifications (GNVQ) should ensure that systematic consideration is given in each case to the identification of the main environmental issues affecting the occupational sector in question; these issues should be included in the GNVQ specifications unless there are very strong reasons to the contrary (paragraph 6.45).

The Employment Department, in concert with the Department of the Environment, should provide support for the Council for Occupational Standards and Qualifications in Environmental Conservation (COSQUEC) to facilitate the speedy completion of its proposed programme of work with other Lead Bodies to encourage the wider and more consistent adoption of integrated environmental competence standards across all relevant occupational sectors (paragraph 6.49).

The scope for enhancing the coverage of environmental issues within A and AS level syllabuses should be considered by the School Examinations and Assessment Council and the Examining Boards (paragraph 6.50).

All professional institutions should seriously assess – or, as the case may be, reassess – the place of environmental issues within those HE courses for which they control or influence the curricula, and take action to promote the appropriate changes (paragraph 6.55).

Introduction

1. We were appointed by Education Ministers in the late summer of 1991, to review the current provision of environmental education in FHE in England and Wales, and identify priorities for its future development, with particular reference to the present and likely future needs of the workforce. Our full terms of reference will be found in Annex A.

Our methods of work

2. We have held five full meetings, including a two-day residential meeting. Much of our work has been undertaken through sub-groups. At our first meeting, we appointed one sub-group to consider the need for environmental education and training as viewed by employers, and another to survey current provision and recent developments within FHE. In the light of their reports, we appointed three further sub-groups to look more closely at the key issues of 'specialist' environmental course provision, updating provision for those already in the workforce and what we have termed 'cross-curricular greening'. Sections 4-6 of our Report are based largely on the work of these sub-groups. The membership of the Committee and each sub-group is listed in Annex B.

3. We were asked to report within a year. Within that timetable, we have consulted with employers, FHE and other interests as widely as was practicable. Most of our consultations were carried out by correspondence on behalf of our sub-groups, and are referred to as appropriate in the body of our report. As will be seen from Annex B, however, representatives of relevant interests attended some sub-group meetings by invitation; and we also held a special meeting in March 1992 to enable representatives of five national organisations (the Confederation of British Industry, Business in the Environment, the Institution of Environmental Sciences, the Council for Environmental Education and the National Union of Students) to present their views orally and discuss them with members of the Committee.

Our remit

4. While we discuss the interpretation of certain other aspects of our terms of reference later, it will be as well to explain at the outset how we understand the expression 'environmental education within FHE'. We have taken 'education' to refer to any course or other learning opportunity provided by an institution within the FE or the HE sector as defined in the *Further and Higher Education Act 1992*. That is to say, we have not sought to distinguish between 'education' and 'training'.

5. 'Environmental', depending on its context, can bear very many different shades of meaning. For our purposes, however, we have interpreted it in terms of the 'agenda' outlined more fully in Section 1 below. On that basis, an issue is 'environmental' if it relates to:

    ● the responsible and sustainable use and re-use of natural resources, biological and physical;

    ● the prevention and/or control of local and global environmental pollution;

    ● the conservation and sustainable management of the natural environment;

    or any combination of these.

6. This means, for example, that we have not looked at education and training which relates purely to workplace health and safety (while recognising that some workplace hazards have implications for the 'external' environment). We have likewise excluded from our purview issues relating purely to the visual qualities of the environment. In relation to architectural education, for example, our concern has been not with the aesthetics of building design, but with the attention which architecture courses give – or fail to give – to such questions as energy efficiency in buildings and the relative 'greenness' of different building materials.

7.   There is one other area of provision which we have excluded from the scope of our Report, notwithstanding its importance and the concerns which some of us might have wished to express about it. Paragraphs 17.43–44 of the 1990 White Paper *This Common Inheritance*[1] acknowledged the need for initial and in-service teacher training to support the development of environmental education within the National Curriculum, and indicated the steps being taken to promote this. We could see nothing in our terms of reference – literally construed – to preclude us from assessing the need for further action on this front, given that teachers are part of the 'workforce' whose needs we were invited to consider. But it would have been difficult to address these teacher training issues without engaging in a substantive discussion of the National Curriculum itself, and this would have carried us into territory which we assume that our remit was not intended to cover.

Other points of terminology

8.   Two other points of terminology call for comment. First, our frequent metaphorical use of the word 'green' and its cognates. Since this word is often (though by no means invariably) associated with the radical environmentalist viewpoint mentioned in paragraph 1.5 below, we need to emphasise that we have used it ourselves simply as a convenient shorthand expression[2] and not as a polemical slogan. In this connection, it is worth adding that all our recommendations are, in our view, fully compatible with the assumptions underlying *This Common Inheritance*.

9.   Second, we should note that 'universities', in this Report, refers to those institutions which were universities at the *outset* of our enquiry in 1991. As a corollary, we sometimes refer to 'polytechnics'. Since we began work, the title 'university' has of course been conferred on virtually all of the latter. But at certain points,

1. *This Common Inheritance: Britain's Environmental Strategy*, Department of the Environment. HMSO, London 1991 Cm 1200.

2. Its advantages can be seen if the shorthand phrase 'cross-curricular greening' is compared with the more accurate, but very ponderous, expression 'environmental education for the student body at large'.

we have needed to draw broad distinctions between the state of environmental education in the (pre-1992) universities as a class and the (ex-)polytechnics as a class, and the old nomenclature has enabled us to avoid some awkward phraseology.

Nature of this report

10. We have mentioned the timescale within which we were asked to work. This has restricted our scope for detailed research, and in outlining what we believe to be the way ahead, we are far from claiming to have said the last word. But we are glad we were asked to work fast. Despite the significant progress made by a minority of pioneering institutions, environmental education is in many respects badly underdeveloped within FHE, and the urgent need is not for last words but for first steps. The available evidence is, we believe, more than sufficient to suggest what these should be.

1 Education and the environmental agenda

Main points

- Scientific advances have greatly enlarged the 'environmental agenda', both in terms of the magnitude of the issues now seen to be at stake, and in terms of their implications for human activities hitherto taken for granted.

- This agenda must be addressed, notwithstanding the many difficult choices which will have to be made.

- If it is to be addressed effectively, far greater environmental understanding must be developed across the population at large.

- The formal education system shares this task with other parties, but its role is a major one which must be developed despite the sensitive issues which may arise in the process.

The environmental agenda

'Ever since the Age of Enlightenment, we have had an almost boundless faith in our own intelligence and in the benign consequences of our actions. Whatever the discoveries of science, whatever the advances of commerce and industry, whatever the rate at which we multiplied as a species, whatever the rate at which we destroyed other species, whatever the changes we made to our seas and landscape, we have believed that the world would stay much the same in all its fundamentals. We now know that this is no longer true'. (*This Common Inheritance*, paragraph 1.8)

1.1   This quotation from the 1990 White Paper on the environment captures the essence of the contemporary 'environmental agenda'. Concern for the environment is not new. It has influenced public policy in Britain at least since the mid-19th century, when the first Public Health Acts were passed and the Alkali Inspectorate (forerunner of HM Inspectorate of Pollution) was established. But until recently, public policy – and public debate – reflected a narrow conception of environmental responsibility. Environmental protection, on this view, was essentially concerned with the restriction of activities judged to be locally damaging to health, amenity, or both.

1.2   This narrow conception is no longer tenable. Local environmental protection has lost none of its importance; in some respects it presents greater challenges than ever. But the local issues must now be seen as items within a very much wider environmental balance-sheet, on which the bottom line is the planet's capacity to sustain life. To quote again from the White Paper: 'We may not be seeing the end of Nature. But Nature is certainly under threat'.

1.3   Items on the contemporary environmental agenda include such issues as global warming, ozone depletion, the maintenance of biodiversity, and the potential exhaustion of some of the earth's non-renewable resources. In scientific terms, each issue is surrounded by its own margin of uncertainty. What has, however, become increasingly clear is our dependence on a global complex of environmental systems which are far more delicately-balanced, and require far closer care and maintenance, than centuries of human activity have tacitly assumed. Against this background, the uncertainties will sometimes serve only to strengthen the case for precautionary action.

1.4   Providing the necessary care and maintenance may call for changes in many areas of human activity which can now be seen to put the environment at risk by treating it wrongly as an infinite resource – in terms of what is taken out of it, or in terms of the waste and pollution which it can absorb. For example, manufacturers can no longer assume that their environmental obligations are discharged simply by adopting 'clean' and energy–efficient production technologies and ensuring that their goods are 'safe in use'. For many firms, a serious commitment to environmental responsibility may raise difficult questions about the selection and sourcing of their materials and the ultimate disposal of their products. Nor can these issues be seen simply in terms of corporate responsibility. What firms can afford to produce depends in the last analysis on what customers want to consume, and the price they are willing to pay.

1.5 There is a consensus of responsible opinion that 'we cannot go on like this'. Beyond this consensus lies an area of sharp controversy – with ethical as well as scientific dimensions – about what must be done, on what timescale, and at whose short-term expense (nationally and internationally). On one view, what is called for is essentially prudent restraint. Others argue that the achievement of 'sustainable development' will require very drastic changes in lifestyles; changes which themselves imply a radical trans-formation of society's values and renewal of some of its institutions.

1.6 It is not our business as a Committee to enter into these controversies. In any case we hold differing shades of opinion as individuals. But we can all endorse the following key points, which are clearly acknowledged in *This Common Inheritance* :

- the environmental agenda will not go away;

- it affects everybody;

- it involves difficult and potentially painful choices;

- we have no option but to address it.

These premises are more than sufficient to serve as a starting-point for our enquiry.

The role of education

1.7 Responsibility for addressing the environmental agenda is widely diffused: it is an individual responsibility as well as a collective one. Regulation and compulsion cannot achieve all that is required; they are in any case acceptable, in a democracy, only if the need for them is sufficiently widely acknowledged. This implies a need to raise the level of environmental awareness across the population at large and promote far wider understanding of:

- the way the planet's life-sustaining systems function (at least in outline);
- the importance of maintaining the delicate balance of these systems by living in harmony with them, and the skills which this will require;

- the reasons why 'non-sustainable' activities come about, and the contribution which the individual makes to them.

1.8   This is a common task involving many parties besides the formal education system. Self-evidently, however, education has a major role. It is a role which involves some sensitivities, which we must acknowledge.

1.9   First, sustainability is not attainable by knowledge alone. It involves acceptance of what *This Common Inheritance* described as 'the ethical imperative of stewardship'. This in turn implies the development of a heightened sense of personal and collective responsibility, in relation both to future generations and to other people (maybe on the other side of the world) here and now. There are values at the heart of the environmental agenda; and, as often where values are involved, there are differing views about the proper educational response. There are those who cast environmental education in an overtly evangelistic role; at the other end of the spectrum are those who see serious dangers of simplistic one-sidedness, unless environmental education gives values a wide berth and restricts itself to the scientific issues.

1.10   We find ourselves, as individuals, located at various points on this spectrum. We would, however, all agree that, insofar as education seeks to lead opinion, it will do so more effectively if it keeps in mind the distinctive nature of its mission, which is first and foremost to improve its students' *understanding*. Their *concern* may well be awakened as a result; but it must be a properly informed concern. This does not necessarily mean treating 'the environment' as a purely 'scientific' issue. It does mean clearly distinguishing the respective roles of science and ethics, and acknowledging the complexities of each. Failure to do this may lead all to readily to an 'environmentalism' which, by depicting possibilities as certainties, can only discredit itself in the long run and feed the complacency which it seeks to dispel.

1.11   There are other sensitivities, of a more strictly 'academic' kind. The environmental agenda challenges many of the ways in which we look at the world – and have been taught to look at it. Implementation of the desired solution to a particular environmental problem may involve the application of a single scientific discipline. The choice of solution – and indeed the definition of the problem – may require insights from several. Economics can help in certain ways with the choice of solutions; but as traditionally practised it embodies assumptions which (in their very limited conception of environmental costs and benefits) are arguably part of the problem.

1.12   This implies the need for a level of collaboration between disciplines which challenges traditional, compartmentalised academic structures. There may also be a need to redefine the boundaries of some of the disciplines themselves. The achievement of a really thoroughgoing interdisciplinarity in the study of the environment raises issues which we have not attempted to explore in depth; they are difficult issues (at least if the disciplinary babies are not to go out with the bath-water), and radical change – even if judged to be desirable – will not be attainable in short order. There is, nevertheless, real scope here and now for encouraging students to set their disciplines in their wider environmental context, and we believe that FHE should be making every effort to exploit the available opportunities.

1.13   For more than one reason, therefore, environmental education has a delicate path to steer. Some of its practitioners have doubtless made mistakes (of whatever kind) in the past, and some of them will doubtless do so in the future. But this – which could in any case be said of many other areas of education – provides no good ground for inaction. We have said that the environmental agenda will not go away. Nor will it wait. Education must do what it properly and practicably can to help us address it.

2 The needs of the workforce

Main points

- The 'environmental agenda' will impact increasingly on all areas of economic activity.

- In terms of the workforce's need for environmental knowledge, skills and awareness, the implications are considerable.

- Individual needs will vary very widely, but a basic level of knowledge and awareness should be expected across the workforce as a whole.

2.1 We emphasised in paragraph 1.7 that the achievement of sustainability will depend, among other things, on the development of considerably greater environmental awareness, understanding and responsibility across the population as a whole. Our remit, however, is cast in terms of the 'knowledge, skills and awareness which the *workforce* will need'. As we shall suggest in paragraph 6.7 below, this implied distinction is in some important respects artificial; but so far as we have been able, we have focussed our work accordingly.

2.2 Even viewed in this perspective, the field is very broad. Although employers[1] vary in their awareness of what is likely to be expected of them, the 'environmental agenda' will impact increasingly on all areas of economic activity. Its demands will be expressed in many ways, through public and 'green consumer' pressure as well as government and European Community policies pursued through a range of instruments including direct regulation, the provision of fiscal and economic (dis)incentives and maybe measures to extend polluters' liabilities under civil law. These national and EC policies will often be influenced by wider international agreements.

2.3 All this will have implications extending well beyond the more obviously 'dirty' industries (and their increasingly vigilant and liability-conscious insurers and bankers). Every form of economic activity has a potentially adverse impact on the environment,

1. Throughout this report, 'employers' should be understood to include (where appropriate) self-employed persons, whether or not they themselves employ others.

24

whether it causes 'pollution' (in the traditional sense) or not. Not necessarily an unacceptable impact, taking one consideration with another. But in terms – for example – of resources used and waste created, improved environmental performance will find its way onto the agendas of a widening range of organisations (including FHE institutions!), by no means all of whom have yet realised that they have an 'environmental performance' to improve.

2.4 Given the almost infinite variety of circumstances, the 'knowledge, skills and awareness' needed to rise to this challenge can be mapped only in fairly broad terms. This is attempted – from two different angles – in the boxes below.

A. Environmental knowledge/skills/ awareness required by the workforce

a. a general awareness of the importance of environmental issues (global and local) and the need for responsible environmental stewardship

b. awareness of the ways in which the activities of the individual's organisation are liable to impact upon the environment.

c. an appreciation of the individual's own potential contribution to the environmental performance of his/her organisation

d. the capacity to detect (and preferably anticipate) specific situations, arising from the organisation's activities, which may give rise to the need for preventive or remedial measures

e. an appreciation of the full range of costs and benefits likely to result from responding (or not responding) to the situations identified at d.

f. the ability, where problems have been identified, to design solutions which reflect a holistic appreciation of the environmental context (and which do not therefore create new problems in solving the old ones)

g. the necessary knowledge, skills and understanding to implement agreed solutions, and generally to maintain good ongoing environmental practice within the organisation.

B. Environmental roles within the workforce

An environmentally competent workforce will need to comprise the following three classes of personnel:

Environmental *practitioners:* typically scientists, engineers and technicians whose functions within their organisations include the control or monitoring of processes and operations which are liable to affect the environment adversely

Environmental *co-ordinators:* managers whose responsibilities include the development and co-ordination of environmental strategies for their organisations

Environmentally *responsible individuals:* individuals·who possess certain basic standards of environmental awareness, together with an adequate appreciation of the environmental impact of their own work and of the ways in which they can minimise its adverse effects. This category should be understood to include the whole workforce, *including* the practitioners and co-ordinators.

2.5 The list in Box A reflects the needs of the workforce collectively. For the individual, the relevance of each item will depend on the nature of his/her organisation, and on his/her role within it. On this latter point, Box B sets out – with some slight modifications – a very helpful classification suggested in a recent Scottish report[2]. This classification – which will recur frequently in our own report – was intended for industry and commerce, but seems broadly transferable to other sectors, albeit with some differences of emphasis. In a nature conservation body, for example, we would regard *most* of the staff (except the office staff) as practitioners, at least for some of the time, although many of their skills may be practical rather than technical, and their activities will be rather different from those suggested by the definition in the box.

2. *Towards Environmental Competence in Scotland: Phase 2: Industry in Commerce (*Scottish Enterprise, 1991).

2.6   Although Boxes A and B offer only a very broad sketch of what –
       in terms of individual needs – is a very complex picture, certain
       pointers to the role of FHE emerge very clearly.

2.7   First, the need for 'environmental responsibility' (in the terms of
       Box B). Individuals' *scope* for environmental responsibility will
       clearly vary. It may be largely confined to the mundane disciplines
       of turning off lights or using paper economically, or it may involve
       taking detailed account of environmental factors in the context,
       for example, of major decisions on procurement or design. The
       implications – in terms of knowledge, skills and awareness – will
       vary accordingly. But it seems fair to suggest that what is needed,
       across the workforce as a whole, is *at least* the same level of
       consciousness as is nowadays expected of employers and
       employees in such areas as health and safety or equal
       opportunities; and for very many members of the workforce a good
       deal more than this will be required. The whole FHE student body
       should therefore be seen, in principle, as a target-group for some
       form of environmental education.

2.8   Second, the 'practitioners' and 'co-ordinators' of the future cannot
       necessarily be identified as *distinct* target-groups, at least at the
       stage of their initial education[3]. This particularly applies to
       practitioners and co-ordinators in industry and commerce. As the
       definitions in Box B imply, these individuals may well combine
       their 'environmental' roles with other scientific, technical and
       managerial duties (for which they will have had to acquire
       appropriate qualifications); and in any event they are likely to
       have reached their present positions by many different routes. At
       present, indeed, we suspect that some companies are choosing 'co-
       ordinators' (in particular) in a fairly haphazard way. No doubt
       there will be improvements in this respect. Nevertheless, it is
       likely that industry will continue to recruit most of its
       'practitioners' and 'co-ordinators', albeit more systematically, from
       the ranks of its existing scientific, technical and managerial
       personnel.

       3. By 'initial education' we mean any FE or HE which follows school, either end-
       on or without significant intervening work experience. Its antithesis is
       'continuing education'. The distinction is not clear-cut – courses which primarily
       admit school-leavers may also admit mature students who have been away from
       education for some time – but it is serviceable enough for present purposes.

2.9 Third, the knowledge and skills which individuals will need in respect of items b.–g. in Box A will often be too specific (to the industry, for example, or even the firm) to be practically addressed through initial education, even where the individual's likely need of them can be foreseen. Quite aside from this, there is the need for individual members of the workforce to keep abreast – in whatever degree of detail is in their case appropriate – with developments in scientific knowledge and technological know-how, new legislation, and other factors affecting the way in which they and their organisations will need to discharge their environmental responsibilities.

2.10 So while the classification in Box B is helpful conceptually, it does not correspond to any neat hierarchy of educational need. The development of Occupational Standards and NVQs[4] will provide valuable clarification in certain important areas, but the picture is likely to remain complicated in many respects. Our next section draws out the main implications for the provision of environmental education in FHE, and comments on FHE's response to date.

4. For a background note on NVQs see Annex D. Their main implications for environmental education are considered in paragraphs 4.48–49, paragraphs 6.43–49, and Annex E paragraphs 13–15.

3 The role of further and higher education: an overview

Main points

- FHE's response to the needs of the workforce will need to include specialist qualifying courses, 'updating' for those already in the workforce and the provision of environmental education for the student body at large.

- Specialist course provision appears to be broadly adequate in volume, although the content of some courses may require some adjustment.

- 'Updating' provision, however, is patchy and environmental education for 'non-specialist' students is seriously underdeveloped.

- In addressing these needs, FHE will enjoy much support from employers and students (although dialogue with employers will need to be strengthened).

The current situation

3.1 From what we have said in paragraphs 2.7—10, it is not too difficult to infer that FHE's response to the needs we have identified must have three main strands, namely:

a. *specialist, qualification-bearing courses* concerned either with the study of the environment as such, or with specific aspects of environmental conservation, protection and management (paragraphs 4.1—2 explain more fully how we define this strand)

b. working with industry, commerce and other employment sectors to identify the needs of those already in the workforce for environmental knowledge, understanding, awareness and skills, and providing *'updating' courses and other learning opportunities* to meet the needs identified

c. the provision of *appropriate environmental education for the student body at large* (whether through the medium of their specialist subjects or otherwise).

Specialist qualification-bearing courses

3.2 This aspect of our remit was highlighted in paragraph 17.49 of *This Common Inheritance*, which referred to the supply of, and demand for, 'environmental courses and qualifications'. Underlying paragraph 17.49, we assume, was a fear of shortfalls in supply. In fact, most forms of specialist provision have been expanding fairly rapidly. At least some of this expansion seems to have reflected optimistic assumptions about the environment-related employment opportunities likely to be available, and there is a need for the institutions concerned to look closely at their course objectives and curricula.

3.3 Conversely, we have uncovered very little firm evidence of current or imminent shortages, and while we expect an increase in demand for certain kinds of specialist course, we would expect FHE to be willing and able to respond. However, there is sufficient uncertainty surrounding future trends to call for some vigilance.

Updating

3.4 The present level of activity varies widely between institutions. To some extent this is as it should be. Institutions, particularly perhaps in FE, differ considerably in their range and level of relevant specialist expertise, and employers vary widely in their awareness of their own needs. But we are in no doubt that FHE as a whole should be aiming to step up its involvement significantly, bearing in mind the likely increase in demand, and even allowing for the competition which institutions will face from other course providers.

Environmental education for the student body at large

3.5 Of the strands specified in paragraph 3.1, this is by far the least well-developed, despite some pockets of excellent practice. Few FHE institutions have addressed the issue in a co-ordinated way, and it has received relatively little attention from examining, validating, and professional bodies. It requires far higher priority.

3.6 We recognise the sensitivities involved in suggesting that the environmental dimension should feature much more prominently in the generality of FHE curricula. But FHE must surely give serious thought to its role in preparing students to take their place in a world of work where they will be increasingly expected to think and act as 'environmentally responsible individuals'; and insofar as the typical 'co-ordinator' or 'practitioner' will often need to be a 'green engineer' (or accountant, or chemist, or whatever) rather than somebody trained from the start as an 'environmental specialist', this must surely have implications for his or her initial education. At present, however, environmental issues are widely ignored, even in vocational courses to which they are clearly relevant. Just *how far* the environment should permeate curricula in FHE may be a matter for debate: but we are clear - and so are many major employers – that the process should be carried a great deal further than it has been to date.

The way ahead

3.7 In the remainder of this report, we look more closely at the three strands set out on page 29, and indicate the broad lines on which each strand should be further developed. There are a number of points on which we see the need for action nationally, but progress will depend above all on action at institutional level. In responding to the challenge, we are clear that FHE will have the support of both its student and its employer clients.

3.8 Student interest is being expressed in many ways. Demand for 'specialist' courses is buoyant; within other courses, environment-related options and projects are popular. There is much student union activity. Attitudes will vary, and an interest in extra-curricular environmental activities may not imply the same enthusiasm for the addition of substantial and demanding environmental elements to crowded course programmes, but we are in no doubt that the developments recommended in this Report go broadly with the grain of student expectation, and that students themselves are a resource to be drawn on in bringing these developments about.

3.9 Employers increasingly recognise the part which the 'environmental agenda' is going to play in a wide range of business decisions affecting, for example, procurement and marketing as well as production processes. For most firms, compliance with the demands of national and EC legislation is still the main preoccupation. But there are often commercial advantages to be gained by improved environmental performance, in terms of a firm's image with consumers and investors as well as its energy and materials costs. These are becoming more widely appreciated. The adoption of corporate environmental policies is a conspicuous trend, which will receive further impetus from such developments as the proposed EC Eco-Audit Regulation and the new British Standard for Environmental Management Systems (BS 7750). Our own enquiries of employers, and the evidence we received from the CBI, revealed much support for environmental education in FHE.

3.10 We must stress that few of the employers we consulted had reached the stage of articulating their expectations of the education system in any detail. As we shall need to emphasise more than once, dialogue between FHE and industry on environmental issues requires much more attention on both sides. Moreover, our enquiries were largely confined to major companies: we might have had a different response from the generality of small and medium-sized enterprises, who are likely, as a class, to be far less well aware of their environmental obligations, let alone their training needs. But there is clearly much employer goodwill, which will spread progressively as industry as a whole becomes more environment-conscious.

3.11 We have one other general point, before turning to detail. We recognise that this Report comes at a challenging time for FHE. The reorganisation taking place under the *Further and Higher Education Act* 1992 will place heavy demands on senior institutional management, particularly in FE – which faces the additional challenge of restructuring many of its courses in response to the introduction of NVQs. Institutions can also expect continuing pressure from their Funding Councils to achieve reductions in their unit costs. But none of this, in our view, provides cause for inaction. It is important to be realistic about the pace at which environmental education can be expected to develop within FHE; but realism is not the same thing as defeatism, and some institutions have shown that it is possible to make a meaningful start. We see no reason why others should be unable to do likewise.

4 Specialist environmental courses leading to qualifications

Main points

- Current 'specialist' provision ranges widely and includes courses (at all levels) which are geared more or less closely to the requirements of particular environmental occupations, as well as courses (very largely at first degree level) with broader educational objectives.

- Course titles are often opaque and unhelpful to *employers*

- *Student* demand is generally buoyant. Relative to employer demand, however, there is in general no evidence of any quantitative shortfall in provision at present.

- Some increase in employer demand is likely for persons with specialist environmental qualifications at postgraduate and sub-degree level: and also, quite possibly, for holders of vocationally focussed first degrees in such subjects as Environmental Technology.

- We would expect FHE to be able to meet this increase in demand, but the situation should be monitored (particularly in relation to postgraduate courses), and some further research into employer needs may be desirable.

- Broadly based degree courses in Environmental Science and Environmental Studies have a potentially important part to play in the development of an environmentally responsible workforce. In many cases, however, there is need for a careful reappraisal of course content and objectives in the light of the employment opportunities actually available. There is also a need to ensure that graduates' capabilities are more widely understood by employers, particularly in industry.

- Some existing syllabuses, at least in FE, will require significant modification to meet NVQ requirements.

- More flexible methods of course-delivery are needed, particularly in the case of postgraduate courses; flexibility will in any case be at a premium where NVQs are involved.

Definitions

4.1 To address this aspect of our remit, we need first to define what we mean by a 'specialist environmental course'. On a broad view, this expression *could* be taken to include very many successful courses in well-established disciplines, such as Biology or Geography, which have an important contribution to make to our understanding of the environment. However, the range of provision embraced by such a definition would be too heterogeneous for useful analysis, and we have therefore defined 'specialist courses' more narrowly, to mean courses which are principally designed:

　a. to develop their students' understanding of the environment, drawing on a *range* of disciplines from the natural sciences, the social sciences, or both; and/or

　b. to provide vocational education for particular kinds of 'environmental practitioner'.

4.2 These categories are not watertight (hence the 'and/or'). A course may have implicit vocational objectives, even if its formally stated aims are purely educational. Conversely, a course with quite specific vocational objectives will have educational outcomes valid in other contexts, not necessarily work-related. In general, however, Environmental Science or Environmental Studies courses seem to us to belong in category a. Falling more or less clearly under b. are courses in Environmental Technology, Environmental Management and the rather special case of Environmental Health; many of the postgraduate courses discussed in paragraphs 4.31—44; courses (mainly FE) in Countryside Management, Countryside Conservation and the like; and courses for professional qualifications, such as diplomas of the Institute of Water and Environment and Institute of Waste Management Diplomas (Annex E, paragraph 3).

Labour market demand

4.3 The available evidence on demand is surveyed in Annex E, and we need only summarise the main points here. In general, a demand for persons with a specific qualification will arise where the knowledge and skills required for a particular kind of work have been defined, either formally by a standard-setting body such as a professional institution or Lead Body[1], or by an informal consensus among employers. Many occupational roles in the environmental field, however, are still embryonic and ill-defined; and even where roles are relatively well-developed (as in conservation work), holders of specialist qualifications – as defined above – may face strong competition from other job applicants.

4.4   Except possibly in some areas of consultancy and local authority work, therefore, it is hard to identify many jobs for which a specialist environmental qualification has up to now been indispensable; and many industrial employers view such qualifications – or at any rate those at the 'broader' end of the spectrum – with scepticism. Not surprisingly, therefore, we have detected no clear current or recent shortages, except in the special case of Environmental Health[2]; and while some increase in employer demand can be foreseen in certain areas, we see no strong grounds for expecting this to exceed the FHE system's capacity to respond.

4.5   In saying this, however, we are very much reliant on what employers have told us about their current perceptions. *Latent* demand is by its nature far more difficult to define, let alone quantify. As noted in Annex E paragraphs 13—15, the development of NVQs should play an important part in converting latent needs into expressed demands, but we believe there may be scope for some complementary research to establish firmer evidence of likely future trends, **and we recommend that the case for such research should be further considered by the Employment Department in consultation with the Department for Education, the Department of the Environment and the Training and Enterprise Councils.**

1. On the role of 'Lead Bodies', see Annex D, paragraphs 2-3.

2. Shortgages in one or two scientific disciplines were mentioned to us by employers, but the disciplines in question fall outside our definition of 'specialist environmental'.

4.6 Meanwhile specialist course provision is expanding in response to *student* demand, particularly in HE, and seems likely to continue to do so. In itself this is not necessarily a cause for concern. Education is not job-specific vocational training. In terms of the *course-related* job opportunities available, many current HE courses are surplus to requirements and would disappear if that were the only criterion. The charge of 'over-provision' should not be made too hastily. At the same time, course-providers must be concerned in general terms with their students' eventual employability, and students need to approach their courses with a realistic appreciation of where they are, and are not, likely to lead. With these points in mind, the remainder of this section reviews the provision currently available.

First degree courses

4.7 As with provision at any level, the definition in paragraph 4.1 leaves room for debate at the margins. As a rough guide to the field, the table below lists a representative selection of current first-degree course titles which include the word 'Environmental', together with the number of institutions offering courses in England and Wales in 1988 and (if all proposed courses started as planned) 1992.

Course title	Number of institutions offering courses	
	1988	1992
A Environmental Biology	9	13
Environmental Chemistry	5	8
Environmental Engineering	5	12
Environmental Geography, Geology, Earth Science	1	7
B Environmental Health	5	9
C Environmental Management, Technology, Monitoring, Control, Protection	2	22
D Environmental Science(s)	13	26
Environmental Studies	8	9

Notes:

(1) The information in this table has been derived from the University Central Council on Admissions (UCCA) and the Polytechnics Central Admissions Systems (PCAS) handbooks for the years in question.

(2) Joint Honours degrees have been excluded, as have modular degree schemes except where these can lead to the award of a 'named' degree in the subject stated.

(3) The table includes courses with titles which are minor variants on those stated. For example, the 'Environmental Science(s)' figure includes all institutions offering courses whose titles include the words 'Environment(al)' and 'Science(s)'; while 'Environmental Engineering' includes 'Civil and Environmental Engineering' (but not 'Civil Engineering').

4.8 The Table excludes the 'traditional' disciplines mentioned in paragraph 4.1, and also a small number of courses which arguably fall within the definition in paragraph 4.1 a.–b. but which do not use the word 'Environmental' in their titles; these include courses in Ecology, Rural Resource Management and Human Ecology (one course). In terms of the classification in the Table, we would assign these courses respectively to Groups A, C and D.

4.9 It is also important to emphasise that the courses included in the Table have been classified according to their titles[3]. While we believe that the resulting groups and sub-groups are reasonably homogeneous overall, a close analysis of the content of each course might well have led us to classify some individual courses differently (particularly at the borderlines between Groups C and D). Within the groups and sub-groups, moreover, some ambiguities of nomenclature should be noted. Thus:

a. 'Environmental Engineering' usually refers to a version of Civil Engineering, but is occasionally used as a virtual synonym

3. Except in the case of one course which is titled 'Environmental Science' but leads to a degree approved either by the Institution of Environmental Health Officers or the Institute of Housing, depending on the option chosen by the student. We have classified this course as 'Environmental Health' (the Housing option is not, of course, directly relevant to our concerns).

for Building Services Engineering (a quite different subject);

b. some 'Environmental Management' courses deal with the conservation and management of the living environment; but one or two use this title in its 'industrial' sense (pollution control, etc).

We return to the general issue of nomenclature below.

Characteristics of current provision

Group A: Environmental Biology, Environmental Chemistry (etc)
Group B: Environmental Health
Group C: Environmental Management, Environmental Technology (etc)

4.10 We need comment only briefly on these three Groups. Group A, indeed, falls at best on the margins of our definition of specialist provision; as their titles imply, most courses in this Group are closely – sometimes very closely – related to long-established disciplines, and their *distinctive* strengths and weaknesses, in labour-market terms, are therefore difficult to assess on the limited information available[4]. Nor have we looked in detail at Environmental Health provision (Group B); Environmental Health Officers (EHOs) have important responsibilities for pollution monitoring, but much of their work relates to issues, such as food hygiene – which are not 'environmental' in our sense of the expression (Introduction, paragraph 5).

4.11 Environmental Health does, however, usefully illustrate the hazards involved in using central controls to match supply with employer demand. On the basis of projections reflecting a fall in demand for EHOs, the former National Advisory Body for Local Authority Higher Education (NAB) carried out a review of provision in polytechnics and colleges which led in 1985 to the

4. For most of these disciplines, an adequate assessment of graduate destinations is in any case difficult because of the small numbers so far involved.

closure of two courses and intake restrictions elsewhere. By the time NAB's recommendations took effect, employer demand was rising again and there were now signs of a shortage, to which HE's response remained muted until the *Education Reform Act* 1988 freed polytechnics and colleges to determine their own priorities. (Provision has since expanded markedly, inhibited mainly by problems concerning the availability of 'sandwich' placements for the students.)

4.12   As will be seen from the Table, most courses in Group C are very new. In general, they appear to have been designed – after varying degrees of consultation with employers – to meet the needs of particular kinds of 'environmental practitioner', either in industry or in the conservation and management of the natural environment. In that sense they are more overtly vocational and sharply targetted than those in Group D, although (as noted in paragraph 4.9) there may be some exceptions to this generalisation. As yet there is little firm evidence on which to judge their success: most of the courses have yet to produce their first graduates, and hardly any have produced more than one cohort. Nor is it possible to assess the latent employer demand which might be brought to the surface if the courses prove to have hit the mark in their needs analysis. Potentially, however, this is an important strand of provision, and there may be room in due course for the further development of courses of this kind by institutions with the necessary expertise.

Group D: Environmental Science and Environmental Studies

4.13   This is the largest strand of provision at first degree level. Most courses of this kind describe themselves as 'interdisciplinary', and while this expression may be a misnomer in some cases[5], their

5. The term 'interdisciplinary' is sometimes loosely used in relation to courses (not only environmental) which would better be described as 'multidisciplinary'. The difference lies in the extent to which a course makes integrated use of its constituent disciplines in problem-solving and aims to develop its students' understanding of the nature of each discipline, in terms of its methodological assumptions and limitations (as distinct from treating each discipline as a resource to be drawn on ad hoc). To ensure the proper integration of different disciplinary perspectives, a truly 'interdisciplinary' course is likely to involve a good deal of collaboration and teamwork, both in teaching and in learning.

curricula make use of a range of traditional disciplines to develop their students' environmental understanding. Their publicity tends to make much of the environmental career opportunities open to graduates, and most students probably hope to go into environment-related work. Compared with courses in Environmental Management or Environmental Technology, however, most of these courses are less closely focussed on *specific* career outlets, although they may include options with a vocational orientation, particularly in their final year.

4.14 Despite these common features, courses differ markedly:

- in their contributing disciplines, and their relative prominence. Most 'Environmental Studies' courses are based largely in the biological and/or social sciences, while 'Environmental Science' implies a natural science base: but the distinction is not clear-cut, and within the natural sciences the balance between physical, biological and earth science varies from course to course;

- in the range of options available, and the time allowed for them. Some courses restrict the scope for optional specialisation, at least until their final year; others offer a range of 'pathways' which diverge at an early stage, with a relatively limited mandatory core for all students;

- in the extent to which their various options and pathways are designed (explicitly or implicitly) to meet the perceived needs of particular kinds of environmental practitioner;

- in the nature of the work experience opportunities (if any) provided as part of the course.

4.15 An obvious question is whether this degree of variety is desirable. It is certainly a source of potential confusion to employers (and maybe students); we return to this in paragraphs 4.25-30 below. But there may also be educational arguments for a measure of 'convergence' around a common core designed to ensure, for example, that students on social science-based courses achieve a specified level of 'literacy' in the natural sciences while natural science-based courses include some socio-economic consideration of the underlying human causes of environmental degradation. Without a very detailed scrutiny of current curricula, the implications of this are difficult to assess; moreover the present variety of provision has positive features which are well worth preserving. But the idea merits serious consideration, and **we commend it to the attention of the Committee of Heads of Environmental Sciences.**

4.16   Judged against their stated objectives, Environmental Science and Environmental Studies courses in the polytechnics and colleges have been found by Her Majesty's Inspectorate of Schools (HMI) to be generally well organised and taught[6]. We believe the same to be true in the universities. We also believe that courses of this kind have the potential to produce graduates capable of making a valuable contribution in many capacities across a range of employment sectors. While they may lack the depth of specialist scientific knowledge sometimes needed by environmental practitioners in industry, for example, one might expect them to be useful in 'generalist' posts (from which they might develop into environmental co-ordinators). Moreover, a course which involves collaborative project work, and requires its students to deal articulately with concepts from more than one discipline, should be very effective in developing certain transferable inter-personal and communication skills.

4.17   Unfortunately, this potential has been only very partially fulfilled. Although the picture varies considerably between courses, the annual First Destination Survey (FDS) suggests that many Environmental Science/Studies graduates have experienced difficulty in finding their first jobs, compared with graduates in the great majority of other disciplines. In this respect the general picture is brighter for the universities than for the polytechnics. From both sectors, however, graduates have up to now gravitated strongly to the public and voluntary sectors, with relatively few going into industry and commerce (particularly if the water industry is set aside as a special case).

6. *Environmental Education in Twenty Polytechnics and Colleges* (Department for Education, 1992).

4.18 In part this will reflect the employer perceptions mentioned in paragraph 4.4 and Annex E, paragraphs 5—6. But it also seems to reflect a fairly widespread disinclination on the part of Environmental Science graduates to consider industrial careers. We have no evidence that courses have set out to inculcate these somewhat negative attitudes (which many students may have brought with them, and which are in any case by no means confined to graduates in this particular subject-area). Still less are we suggesting that students should be discouraged from looking critically at industry's environmental performance. But if Environmental Science/Studies graduates are indeed tending to emerge from their courses with a perspective in which industry is seen *only* as a source of environmental problems, this must be a cause for concern.

4.19 On the question of unemployment, it is right to acknowledge the limitations of the FDS, which reflects the position six months after graduation and may underestimate the *eventual* success of Environmental Science and Environmental Studies graduates in the labour market. But the picture is still disquieting (at least for the polytechnics and colleges), not least because the most recent FDS figures do not (of course) reflect the increase in course intakes which has occurred since 1988. If student demand remains buoyant and HE institutions choose to meet it, the output of Environmental Science and Environmental Studies graduates is likely to rise considerably faster than the employment opportunities in the sectors which these students currently favour.

The way ahead

4.20 Some reassessment of current and planned provision is therefore needed. We do *not* suggest a centrally conducted review leading to the imposition of restrictions on the growth of provision. That would be contrary to current policy on the funding of HE, and past exercises of this kind have in any case been dubiously effective, even in dealing with fairly clear-cut mismatches (see paragraph 4.11). But we would hope to see action – mainly at institutional level – on two main fronts.

Course objectives and content

4.21 **We recommend that all HE institutions providing first degree courses in Environmental Science or Environmental Studies should undertake a searching review of their aims and curricula, in the light of their recent graduates' success or otherwise in both the 'environmental' and the 'general' labour markets.** We recognise that some institutions may already have such a review in hand; in principle, indeed, this should happen in the normal course of an HE institution's course review and revalidation cycle. But we believe that in this particular case there is a need for action outside the normal cycle and possibly going beyond what standard procedures would require.

4.22 This recommendation does not imply that all courses should take on a more 'vocational' character, still less that they should all seek to steer their students towards *industrial* careers. There is room for courses which seek primarily to produce articulate and personally competent graduates (with a body of knowledge which they may or may not use directly in their careers), as well as courses more closely related to specialised employment. But the fact remains that most Environmental Science/Studies students seem to enrol for their courses in the hope of becoming practitioners, and most courses, tacitly or overtly, are trying to respond to this aspiration.

4.23 They must, therefore, ask themselves how successfully they have been doing so. The implications will vary from course to course. It may simply be a matter of doing more to encourage students to consider the full range of employment options (environmental and non-environmental) for which the course provides a sound preparation as it stands; while if changes in the content of the course are desirable, these could be designed to move the course either towards the 'general' or the 'vocational' end of the spectrum. An essential outcome, however, should be a clear and realistic statement of the course's educational and (if any) vocational objectives, and a clear understanding of the contribution which each part of the curriculum is intended to make to each objective.

4.24   While individual institutions must decide which path they wish to take, we would make one specific point. Where courses have offered work experience placements, these have been extremely effective both in opening students' eyes to the opportunities available and in opening employers' eyes to graduates' capabilities. The conversion of a course to the 'sandwich' mode has resource implications, quite apart from possible difficulties in finding an adequate supply of the extended, employer-funded, placements which a sandwich course requires; short unpaid placements, however, are possible under the Awards Regulations subject to certain restrictions. **Where courses do not at present offer placements (of whichever kind), they should seriously consider doing so; where they do, they should explore the scope for increasing the variety of placements offered. Employers, for their part, should make every effort to collaborate with institutions in this.**

Information and guidance for employers

4.25   While changes may be desirable in the emphasis of some current courses, some of the problems we have mentioned are almost certainly the result of misunderstandings. There is justification for some of the employer attitudes which we have mentioned: many 'practitioner' posts in industry, for example, clearly do require a level of specialised scientific knowledge beyond the reach of a typical Environmental Science graduate.

4.26   At the same time, some Environmental Science courses are producing graduates who are more scientifically competent than many employers realise. Faced with job applications from a mixed bunch of graduates, employers understand what the engineers and chemists have to offer; in the case of Environmental Science graduates, they may have no clear picture or, alternatively, an unfavourable perception based on past experience which may not be representative.

4.27   As we have noted, the course-titles 'Environmental Science' or 'Environmental Studies' cover a wide range of provision, and we have mentioned some other ambiguous titles in paragraph 4.9. Too much should not be made of this: an employer seeking an

Environmental Engineer (of either kind!) is unlikely to appoint an Environmental Scientist by mistake. But it cannot be pretended that current course-titles are helpful to the average employer, and **we recommend that the scope for adopting a more consistent nomenclature should be considered by the Committee of Heads of Environmental Sciences, in consultation with the Institution of Environmental Sciences and other relevant interests.** This issue might usefully be considered in conjunction with the question of a 'common core' (paragraph 4.15).

4.28 Even with some rationalisation, however, we recognise that the range of courses – and options – available under such a title as 'Environmental Science' is likely to be considerable. We suggest therefore that providers of such courses should consider issuing each graduate with a 'profile' designed to make it clear to prospective employers what the graduate has actually studied and what level of achievement he or she has reached in each field of study. This must be realistically and accurately done, if it is not to do more harm than good in the long run. But in principle, the idea has merits.

Information and guidance for students

4.29 Equally important is the provision of improved information for prospective students. In relation to individual courses, students will doubtless continue to rely mainly on institutional prospectuses. **It is incumbent on each institution to keep this material under constant review, with particular reference to the accuracy of what it says – or implies – about career outlets.** There may also be scope for improving and systematising the information which is currently available through such national sources as the Educational Counselling and Credit Transfer Information Service.

4.30 Information on individual courses, however, needs to be set in context. Many students, in choosing an 'environmental' course with a view to an 'environmental' career, may have a very limited appreciation of the full range of courses and careers available. Given the existence of a spectrum of provision and a spectrum of career outlets, it is important that students understand just how wide these spectra are, and where their chosen course is located on each spectrum. We make no recommendation, however, because we understand that a handbook with broadly this objective is being prepared by the Institution of Environmental Sciences, with some financial assistance from the Department of the Environment. Pending its appearance, proposals for further action would be premature.

Taught postgraduate courses

4.31 We are concerned in this Section with courses leading to recognised qualifications, and the following paragraphs focus on taught courses leading to MSc degrees and/or Postgraduate Diplomas. Research degree programmes (PhD, MPhil and in some institutions MSc) fall at best on the margins of our remit; research students are of course extending their education as well as conducting research, but we have identified no major issues in this regard. Post-experience courses *not* leading to qualifications - which may be 'postgraduate' in clientele and academic level – are considered in Section 5.

Characteristics of current provision

4.32 As at the undergraduate level, our definition of a 'specialist environmental course' has hazy borderlines with a range of provision in such disciplines as Geology, Agriculture/Horticulture and Engineering. We have however identified about 70 courses in England and Wales which fall pretty clearly within our definition; they include courses in highly specific aspects of environmental technology as well as courses in ecology and conservation. Another 20 or 30 courses could be regarded as borderline (including some which have been designed for developing countries and are not directly relevant to the needs of the United Kingdom workforce).

4.33 The value of specialist postgraduate courses is readily acknowledged by some employers who are, rightly or wrongly, suspicious of 'environmental' first degrees. In this respect, our own information is in line with other recent research[7]. We are therefore dealing with a potentially important area of provision. It is also ill-charted, and we therefore sent a simple questionnaire to 24 HE institutions in respect of 42 postgraduate courses currently provided by them. We received responses in respect of the 30 courses listed in Annex C. A number of points emerge.

4.34   First, this is a rapidly expanding area of provision, particularly at the 'technological' end of the spectrum. In drawing up our sample, we tried (in general successfully) to exclude courses which had been very recently introduced (since they could not have answered some of our key questions). Nevertheless 12 of our 30 courses had been introduced since 1986.

4.35   Since 1990, a stimulus to the development of provision has been provided by the Employment Department's High Technology National Training Programme (HTNT) and its associated Head Office Experimental Programme (HOEP), both of which are part of the Employment Training (ET) Programme. Under HTNT and HOEP, support is provided on ET terms (tuition fees and training allowances) to enable unemployed persons to attend selected courses, leading to recognised qualifications at HNC level or above, in subject-areas for which national need has been identified. Under HOEP – confined to innovative courses which are judged to be potential models of good practice – pump-priming funding is also paid to the institution providing the course. In 1991/92, 16 'environmental' courses (12 MSc/Diploma, four HNC) in England and Wales received HTNT or HOEP support; nine more have been approved for funding in 1992/93. Courses already in existence may apply to participate in HTNT, and several have done so successfully; in a number of cases, however, HTNT/HOEP support has clearly played an important part in getting new provision off the ground.

7. See *The impact of Environmental Management on Skills and Jobs* ECOTEC Research and Consultancy Limited 1990. A brief summary of this report has been published by the Employment Department's Skills and Enterprise Network.

4.36 Student demand is buoyant. Of the courses from which we had responses, a few (mostly very specialised) reported that student applications had been stable over the period 1989–92, but the majority reported significant increases. In eight cases – which included 'ecological' and 'technological' courses – applications were said to have risen by 100% or more. Some institutions noted an improvement in the *quality* of the applicants. A few respondents mentioned the part which the recession had played in generating demand from graduates unable to obtain jobs on the strength of their first degrees, but in general the trend was ascribed to heightened public interest in the environment and was expected to continue, though not necessarily at the same pace.

4.37 On graduate destinations, the general picture seems encouraging. The great majority of our own respondents said that over 75% of students who had completed their courses since 1 January 1990 had found relevant employment (although some of them construed 'relevant employment' rather widely to include, for example, PhD research). For the (mainly new) environmental courses supported through HTNT, most of which we excluded from our own survey, there is little evidence on destinations as yet, but applications for HTNT support must be supported by evidence of employer demand, and HTNT's record in other subject-areas has been generally good.

4.38 Despite the increase in student demand, individual course intakes had increased very little. (Some unsuccessful applicants for admission to our respondents' courses will no doubt have joined new courses elsewhere, but we cannot say how many.) Institutional capacity will doubtless have been the main factor inhibiting the expansion of existing courses, but some respondents referred to problems experienced by students in obtaining financial support, given that postgraduate courses do not attract mandatory awards and Research Council support for students on taught courses is limited.

4.39 Respondents mentioned a range of sources of support for students. The balance varied from course to course, but in general the number of full-time students supported by United Kingdom employers was low. The recession was sometimes cited as a factor.

Some courses admit large numbers of overseas students, although it is unclear how far they have been recruited to fill places which United Kingdom students have found it impracticable to take up (as noted above, some courses were designed with overseas markets in mind). By implication, responses to our questionnaire tend to confirm the significance of HTNT as a source of support. HTNT funding, however, is limited to four years in respect of any course; this could pose eventual problems for the viability of some of the courses supported from this source.

The way ahead

4.40 We hesitate to make too much of these constraints and uncertainties. It can be argued that vocational postgraduate provision should be expected to make its way in the market very largely by attracting employer sponsorship. While we have little doubt that the demand for specialised postgraduate qualifications will increase, our enquiries of employers have revealed no strong evidence of current shortages, nor any firm basis for believing that supply will fail to keep pace with essential demand.

4.41 It would therefore be premature to advocate further central intervention to support the development of new provision. But the situation is clearly a fluid one, and it will be important to deal promptly with any shortages which may appear. **We therefore recommend that the Employment Department, in consultation with the Department for Education, the Welsh Office and the Department of the Environment, should monitor trends in employer demand for persons with postgraduate environmental qualifications, and also keep the development of provision under careful surveillance, to ensure that any shortages or bottlenecks are speedily identified.**

4.42 There may also be ways of making existing provision more accessible, particularly to employer-sponsored students. Modularisation can help in various ways. For example, we were interested to learn of a recently introduced MSc in Integrated Pollution Control which is taught in residential modules of a week or 10 days, supplemented by distance learning. Many employers and their employees might find this pattern attractive by comparison with traditional modes of part-time study (which tend to involve spending one day a week at an institution which may be some distance from home and workplace), and we would encourage other institutions to consider it.

4.43 It has also been suggested to us that post-experience provision is unduly polarised between full-length qualifying courses on the one hand, and very short 'updating' courses on the other. The point was only made to us by one or two employers, but we are sure they have identified an important gap, which modularisation can also help to bridge. We therefore learned with interest of one MSc course which is wholly modularised and attracts large numbers of students who 'sign on' for individual modules without aspiring to the degree. Not all courses will lend themselves to modularisation along these lines, but we suspect that the model could be more widely adopted.

4.44 **We urge HE institutions currently offering – or planning to offer – taught postgraduate courses to take all practicable steps to improve the flexibility of their delivery, whether through the means suggested above or in other ways.**

Provision below first degree level

4.45 Below first degree level, specialist provision (as defined in paragraph 4.1 a.–b.) is currently sparse, and its future development is likely to be much influenced by NVQ requirements. Setting aside a small number of courses for Environmental Health technicians, the main strands to date have been:

a. GCSE and A level courses in Environmental Science or Environmental Studies;

b. vocational courses concerned with the management and/or conservation of the natural environment (more particularly the countryside), mostly run by agricultural colleges and leading to qualifications awarded by the Business and Technology

Education Council (BTEC) or by the National Examinations Board for Agriculture, Horticulture and Allied Industries[8];

c. a (so far) very small number of courses, mainly at BTEC Higher National level, for a clientele which might be (very roughly) characterised as 'environmental technicians'.

4.46 GCSE and A level courses are seen by most students as a rung on the educational ladder (rather than a direct preparation for employment) and we need not comment at length. Two points, however, are worth recording. First – and despite increases in some individual colleges – GCSE and A level entries in Environmental Science/Studies have been static for the last two or three years. In the case of A levels, this may reflect the perceived preference of HE for applicants with 'single subject' qualifications (even where the courses they wish to join are interdisciplinary). Second, we note that proposals for the development of *National Diploma* courses in Environmental Science have been discouraged by BTEC, owing to doubts about the likely career outlets. In view of the problems experienced by some Environmental Science *graduates*, we agree with BTEC.

4.47 Courses in Countryside Management, Countryside Conservation and Countryside Skills have been a significant growth area in the last three years. As noted above, most of these courses are provided by agricultural colleges seeking to diversify their programmes in the face of falling demand for traditional courses in agriculture. The report of the Countryside Commission's Countryside Staff Training Advisory Group[9] was critical of some (*not* all) of these courses, on the basis that they tended to be too strongly focussed on the husbandry skills which the colleges felt able to teach, rather than the skills which the conservation sector actually requires.

8. Reference should also be made to a range of environmental conservation awards offered jointly by City and Guilds and CENTRA, and introduced in 1989/1990. Some 50 public, private and voluntary bodies have been accredited as centres for these awards, including a dozen agricultural and other FE colleges. The awards are essentially practical and were developed, in effect, as interim vocational qualifications pending the introduction of NVQs.

9. *Training for Tomorrow's Countryside* Countryside Commission, 1989.

4.48   We see no need to enter this particular debate: to the extent that these courses *are* out of line with actual needs, they will presumably have to be revised to meet the requirements of COSQUEC's NVQs. We would only add that – whatever view is taken of the quality of current provision – there is little evidence to suggest that it is insufficient in volume. Existing provision, suitably modified, should be adequate to cater for new entrants (at this level) to conservation work; and while existing conservation staff may also wish to acquire the new qualifications, they will not necessarily require a substantial input from FE (Annex E, paragraphs 13–15).

4.49   'Technician' provision (which we use for want of a better expression) is a new development, confined so far to half a dozen HTNT-supported HNC courses in such subjects as Pollution Control, Environmental Management and Energy Conservation, plus (literally) one or two longer-established and successful HND courses. We would expect demand for provision at broadly this level to increase, although we can make no quantitative prediction. If the HTNT students' destinations provide clues, we trust that these will be disseminated by the Employment Department. Patterns of demand are likely to be strongly influenced by NVQs, and we have drawn particular attention in Annex E to the standards and qualifications in Waste Management and Environmental Management which are being developed by the Waste Management Industry Training Advisory Board (WAMITAB) and COSQUEC respectively. Both are likely to provide opportunities for FHE, but it is not yet clear on what scale. Any demand, however, is likely to be for rather more flexible forms of provision than the traditional (H)NC course.

5 Keeping the workforce up to date

Main points

- The workforce's need for environment-related updating is widely recognised in principle by major employers, but the progress they have so far made in identifying their detailed requirements is more variable.

- Among small and medium-sized enterprises, the general level of awareness is likely to be very much lower.

- A substantial increase in demand for updating can be expected as employers appreciate their environmental training needs more clearly.

- FHE will face strong competition from other training providers for a share in this expanding market, but should still be capable of raising its currently very variable levels of activity considerably.

- Not all FHE institutions are equally well-placed to provide environment-related updating, but each institution should make a serious assessment of its potential in this field. Institutions would be assisted in this by having access to case-studies of successful practice.

- Relevant expertise and facilities will be widely dispersed across an institution's departments and faculties. To develop a substantial programme, mechanisms must be in place to mobilise and co-ordinate these resources. Staff development will also be required.

- A considerable improvement in communication between FHE and employers is needed. We doubt whether the national unit proposed in *This Common Inheritance* would be effective in achieving this, but the development of regional and local networks should be strongly encouraged. There is also an important role for Training and Enterprise Councils (TECs).

- Some basic research should be undertaken nationally into the environmental training needs of small and medium enterprises.

General characteristics of 'updating' provision

5.1 Almost any course in FHE may admit mature students, some of whom may have enrolled for reasons related to their work. Our concern in this Section, however, is with vocational education and training which is *specifically* designed to update and improve the knowledge and skills of those already in the workforce. Typically, such 'updating' takes the form of:

a. short courses of (usually) 1–5 days' duration in total;

b. seminars, workshops and conferences;

c. open and distance learning programmes.

5.2 For convenience, we use 'course' to denote all three modes of provision. Some updating courses reflect the very specific needs of a particular client and are provided exclusively for that client: others are marketed and recruit much more widely. Some courses are linked to the 'continuing professional development' (CPD) which professional bodies increasingly expect their members to undertake. Important complementary services, such as trainer training, training needs analysis and consultancy may also be offered by FHE.

5.3 In recent years, FHE has greatly extended its involvement in updating, supported by the Government's PICKUP[1] programme. Selective central funding has been provided – by the Education Departments and more recently by the Universities Funding Council and the Polytechnics and Colleges Funding Council – to help with development and 'infrastructure' costs. Subject to that limited pump-priming, updating courses are expected (at least) to cover their costs by charging economic fees. To succeed on these terms, FHE must be prepared to design courses closely matched in content to the needs of the client, and deliver them at the client's preferred time and venue. This will entail close partnership between institutions and their clients in the planning process;

1. Professional, Industrial and Commercial Updating.

indeed, experts from the relevant industry or other employment sector may sometimes play a major part in the actual teaching of what are, in effect, courses jointly provided by FHE and industry (whether or not they are formally advertised as such).

5.4 There was once a fairly sharp distinction between long courses of initial education which normally led to qualifications, and short updating courses which did not. But this distinction is beginning to break down. As we have noted in paragraph 4.43, modularisation of qualifying courses enables individuals to take single modules to meet immediate work-related needs, at the same time gaining credit (which they may or may not choose later to 'cash') towards a qualification. NVQs will reinforce this trend, designed as they are to be attainable over time by credit-accumulation. This militates against the provision of long courses which are available *only* on an 'all-or-nothing' basis; and candidates for some NVQs may want short, targetted courses quite closely akin to traditional updating (Annex E, paragraph 14). But despite these overlaps, 'updating' remains sufficiently discrete, both as a concept and as an identifiable strand of provision, to require separate examination.

Current supply and demand

5.5 Environment-related updating has a very wide potential coverage in terms of:

- the client-groups for whom it may be provided (shop-floor to senior management and professional staff);

- the topics which it may seek to address (scientific, technical, legal, economic, managerial, etc);

- the range of academic disciplines on which it may need to draw.

Needs will vary markedly from one employment sector to another, and FHE institutions vary almost as widely in the range and level of expertise at their disposal. Clearly, these complexities are not reducible to any simple model of supply and demand.

5.6 To obtain some broad pointers, however, we sought information and advice from 70 employers or employer organisations (mainly, though not exclusively, industrial) and 90 FHE institutions. We are grateful to the 44 employers and 60 institutions who responded. We concentrated our enquiry on those who were likely to have something to tell us: thus most of the employers to whom we wrote were large companies, while our FHE sample was somewhat skewed in favour of institutions known to be actively involved in updating (though not necessarily environmental updating).

Needs

5.7 Most of the updating needs identified by our employer respondents fell fairly clearly under one of four broad heads:

a. general awareness of environmental issues, for *all staff;*

b. a sufficient level of awareness to enable *managers* to recognise the likely environmental impact of their decisions;

c. awareness of the implications of legislation, and the knowledge and skills to comply with it;

d. 'state-of-the-art' knowledge, skills and techniques.

In terms of the classification which we have used elsewhere, the main targets for b. and d. are, respectively, the 'co-ordinators' and 'practitioners' in an organisation; both may have needs under head c. Head a. reflects a recognition of the need for 'environmentally responsible individuals' at all levels of the workforce.

5.8 A more detailed survey of 39 major employers (including 14 of our own respondents) has been carried out by Environmental Resources Limited (ERL) on behalf of Business in the Environment (BiE)[2]. This survey broadly confirms our own findings, although some interesting points of detail emerge. For example, nearly a third of the BiE/ERL survey respondents singled

2. *Survey of Training Needs*: BiE/ERL, April 1992

out 'environmental auditing' as a high priority subject; this may have reflected the stage those firms happened to have reached in the implementation of their corporate environmental policies, and the impact of recent publicity relating to the EC's proposed Eco-Audit Regulation and BS 7750. Conversely, few mentioned waste management, perhaps because the phased introduction of the relevant provisions of the Environmental Protection Act 1990 had yet to affect them directly.

5.9   No doubt the perceived importance of particular topics will continue to fluctuate over time. The 'environmental agenda' is not static. Precisely for that reason, however, most of our respondents, and BiE/ERL's, clearly foresaw an ongoing need for updating, to take account of, for example, changing legislative requirements and new developments in the state of knowledge. This view is shared by the CBI. Only at the level of very 'general awareness' (paragraph 5.7, head a.) is the need for updating expected to diminish over time (so long as the environment receives due attention within initial education).

Current FHE provision

5.10   Most HE institutions who responded to us had been providing 'environmental' updating courses, although the scale of this activity varied considerably. The great majority of the provision reported to us fell within heads b.—d. of paragraph 5.7. This is not surprising; the delivery of general 'awareness training' to large numbers of staff (head a.) is something which major companies may well believe they can undertake more cost-effectively in-house.

5.11   With some exceptions – particularly perhaps in the case of specialist colleges dealing with the land-based industries – FE appears to have been somewhat less active. This is under-standable. HE has a higher level and wider range of relevant scientific expertise at its disposal; moreover major companies seem to be looking to 'external' providers mainly to meet the needs of relatively well-qualified and senior staff, and it is not surprising that they should turn to HE for this. We believe, however, that both sectors have an important contribution to make, not only in the actual provision of courses but also in the process of training needs analysis.

Employers' use of FHE provision

5.12   While there is willingness on the part of many institutions to provide updating in broadly the areas regarded by employers as important, it is not so clear how far employers are currently looking to FHE as the natural provider. In some cases they have been doing so, particularly where the institution concerned has an established reputation for environmental research or consultancy. Many of our FHE respondents, however, had found it necessary to make the first move in approaching employers: of our employer respondents, only a minority had so far used FHE for updating (as distinct from research and consultancy).

5.13   There may be a number of reasons for this. For example:

● even among the relatively environment-conscious employers whom we and BiE/ERL consulted, progress made so far with the identification of training needs is likely to vary considerably. It is worth noting that, while nearly all of the BiE/ERL survey respondents had corporate environmental policies in place, implementation had in many cases only just begun;

● most of our (and BiE/ERL's) respondents were large companies who had the capacity to deliver substantial training programmes in-house (and were in some cases already doing so);

● information on 'external' training provision was said by some BiE/ERL respondents to be hard to come by.

5.14   There is also the question whether the updating currently offered by FHE is sufficiently well-targetted. In fact no complaints were made by those of our respondents who had actually made use of FHE, but reservations were expressed by some of BiE/ERL's survey participants. In particular, the suggestion was made that current courses are more effective in teaching specific techniques, such as auditing, measurement and analysis than in helping managers grapple with the business implications of environmental issues. That is to say, practitioners are better served than co-ordinators. It is not clear how far this criticism was specifically aimed at FHE (as distinct from other providers) or whether it was based on full knowledge of what is available. We cannot therefore readily assess its validity. But the point - insofar as it is valid - is important.

Future potential

5.15   Environmental updating is a complex market in which FHE will need to compete with commercial training providers, major companies' in-house training facilities, and Industry Training Organisations (ITOs). But FHE has significant strengths in terms of its infrastructures and the range of expertise at its disposal, and the market is clearly going to expand. Even in relation to major employers, paragraphs 5.12—14 suggest that FHE's role is underdeveloped compared with its potential. While large firms can provide much of their own training, the implementation of their corporate environmental strategies is likely to reveal specialised requirements which cannot be met in-house. In many ways even more important are the likely needs of small and medium-sized enterprises. Many of these enterprises appear still to be very imperfectly aware of the steps which legislative and other pressures will require them to take to improve their environmental performance; and compared with major companies they are far less well-placed to meet their consequential training needs, or even to identify them, without help from outside.

The way ahead

5.16   It would be unwise to second-guess this still-evolving market by recommending specific priorities; but we are in no doubt of the scope – and in the interests of the environment, the need – for a significant overall expansion in the provision of environmental updating by FHE. The extent of each institution's involvement will vary. Some institutions are well-equipped to enter the market on a broad front; others may wish to concentrate on a limited range of provision reflecting their particular capabilities; others may see no role for themselves. The decision is one which each institution must take for itself. But it should be taken consciously, after some consideration of the options, and not by default. **We therefore recommend that each institution, pursuant to its overall environmental strategy (see Section 7), should carefully consider the scope for extending its involvement in environment-related updating.**

5.17 The remainder of this Section draws attention to a number of issues which will need to be addressed, both by institutions and by other parties, if FHE's potential as a provider of environmental updating is to be fully realised.

Co-ordination at institutional level

5.18 Insofar as the development of environment-related updating presents particular problems by comparison with updating in any other field, these arise from the sheer variety of issues encompassed by the environmental agenda, and the corresponding range of disciplines from which an input may be needed. Effective co-ordination across departments and faculties is therefore vital, if an institution aims to offer more than a narrow range of courses.

5.19 The point here is not that *every* environment-related updating course will need to be multidisciplinary: some needs, particularly at the technological end of the spectrum, can be met through a 'single-subject' approach. Unless someone within the institution is taking an overview, however, these needs may never be brought to the attention of those who might have been able to meet them; and employers enquiring whether the institution might be able to help with a particular training need may be told, incorrectly, that it cannot.

5.20 Some institutions have created multidisciplinary 'environmental units' (albeit in some cases for research and consultancy, rather than training). In many others, central units or other mechanisms have been set up to promote the development of updating provision in general. Whatever precise form they take, however, institutional management must ensure that systems are in place for mobilising and co-ordinating the necessary expertise across the institution, and dealing competently with enquiries from employers. Setting up these systems may require some investment, and **we recommend that environmental updating should be given priority, both by institutions and by the Further and Higher Education Funding Councils, in the allocation of any funds which may be available to support the development of updating in general.**

Institutional environmental practice

5.21 In Section 7 below, we urge all FHE institutions to adopt comprehensive strategies for improving their overall environmental performance. As we argue there, the adoption and implementation of such strategies has educational as well as environmental significance, and the benefits are particularly evident in relation to updating. An institution which sets out to teach environmental auditing, for example, will do so more credibly and effectively if it has first-hand experience of auditing its own operations.

Information and publicity

5.22 Experience in other subject areas suggests that FHE institutions are sometimes better at designing and delivering high-quality updating courses than they are at promoting them. We have already mentioned the difficulties experienced by some employers in tracking down relevant courses. To a great extent – particularly where clienteles are mainly local – the remedy must lie largely with the institutions themselves, although there is also an important role for TECs to play (see paragraph 5.30 below) in developing better communications.

5.23 At the same time, there may be scope for some improvement in the information available nationally, perhaps through the development of a directory covering not only updating, but also the range of other environment-related services which FHE is in a position to provide. We recognise the exceptional problems involved in maintaining a database of short courses which is sufficiently comprehensive and accurate to be useful. **We recommend, nevertheless, that the feasibility of developing**

such a directory should be further examined, in the first instance by the Department for Education in consultation with the Welsh Office.

Dissemination of good practice

5.24 Environment-related updating is, for many institutions, a new area of work. In considering what their own role might be, we are sure that many institutions would find it helpful to have access to some case-studies of good practice illustrating, in particular, the expertise and other resources likely to be needed to ensure the successful design and delivery of different kinds of course. **We recommend that the Department for Education, in consultation with the Welsh Office, should consider how this might best be achieved.** There is also scope for sharing good practice more informally, and we hope that institutions will not feel unduly inhibited from this by fears for their own competitive advantage. On the face of it, there is likely to be more than enough work to go round.

Accreditation

5.25 In relation to short courses, employers tend to use this term in two rather different senses. On the one hand, many employers would welcome the introduction of some mechanism for 'kite-marking' the courses themselves, to help them as prospective customers distinguish the wheat from the chaff. While we sympathise with this plea, we doubt if this form of 'accreditation' is feasible, given the problems involved in subjecting short – and often one-off – courses to meaningful 'vetting'. Some professional bodies have wrestled with this problem with a view to drawing a line between courses which may and may not be 'counted' by members in the context of their CPD obligations, and have found it very intractable.

5.26 In the other sense, 'accreditation' implies that successful completion of the course carries the award of a credit which formally attests a level of competence achieved, and which may count – via systems of credit accumulation and transfer – towards a wider qualification. We are not sure how much importance employers attach to accreditation in this sense, and by no means all short courses take a form which readily allows for meaningful assessment of the students. But it is usually valued by the students themselves, and if a course can be related to a recognised national qualification (an option for which there should be increasing scope as the NVQ system develops), this may go at least some way to meeting the point discussed in our previous paragraph.

Staff development

5.27 Staff development will be needed for two main reasons. The first is pedagogic. Where teaching staff have been mainly engaged in classroom work with young FE students or lecturing to large audiences of undergraduates, they may need help in acquiring the rather less 'didactic' teaching skills required to meet the more sharply focussed expectations of an audience of adults who may have much to contribute to the course from their own knowledge and experience. Institutions involved in any form of updating are already familiar with this need; diversification into new fields of activity will however extend the range of staff requiring help.

5.28 Second, staff engaged in updating need themselves to be fully up-to-date, not only in their specialist subject knowledge, but also in their appreciation of what the client requires. As we noted in paragraph 5.14, the suggestion has been made that course providers are not always good at relating their scientific and technical expertise to the wider business context in which real-life environmental management decisions have to be taken. To the extent that there is substance in this criticism, it is important to address it. Here, the way ahead lies not in formal in-service training, but in the maintenance of dialogue between institutions and their clients, complemented perhaps by staff secondments (either way). **We recommend that all institutions involved in environment-related updating should explore with their industrial and other clients the scope for such secondments.**

Communication between FHE and employers

5.29 Paragraphs 5.18–28 have been largely concerned with the supply side of the environmental updating market. But action is also needed on the demand side, to raise employers' awareness of their environment-related training needs and help them articulate these needs for the guidance of FHE (and other providers). To that extent, we share the concerns which underlay paragraph 17.57 of *This Common Inheritance*. However, it is much less clear to us that these concerns would be best addressed through the mechanism proposed in *This Common Inheritance*: namely, the establishment of 'a new [national] environmental unit within the further and higher education sector to improve communications between education and business country-wide'.

5.30 We have two main reservations about the concept of a special national unit for this particular purpose[3]. First, much of the market for updating is, by its nature, local; and insofar as it is national, many of the demands are specific to particular industrial sectors. Second, we believe that much of the necessary dialogue can and should be developed through channels which already exist. Nationally, Industry Training Organisations are concerned with identifying training needs industry-by-industry (and often 'double' as standard-setting Lead Bodies), while many trade associations play a vital role in briefing their members on environmental issues. Locally, we suspect that the TECs' potential role in promoting environment-related training is underdeveloped. Valuable initiatives have been undertaken by some TECs, but most of these have had a 'conservation' focus (often in the context of specific local environmental projects). We are less clear how far the TECs have yet concerned themselves with the need for greater day-to-day environmental responsibility in industry, and the training needs arising from this. **We would urge the Employment Department and the Welsh Office to encourage them to do so.**

5.31 In these circumstances, we believe that dialogue will be far more effectively promoted through the development of local and regional networks bringing FHE together with the parties we have mentioned, and other relevant interests. We are aware of a number of embryonic networks already established, either through purely local initiatives, or with some encouragement from central

3. The need for other national measures to support the developmnent of environmental education in FHE is considered in Section 7 below.

government. Believing that the case for a national unit is not proven, **we therefore recommend that the Department for Education, the Welsh Office, the Employment Department, the Department of Trade and Industry and the Department of the Environment should urgently consider other ways and means of encouraging better communication between FHE and employers, building on networks and mechanisms which already exist, and bearing in mind the need for arrangements which are sufficiently local in focus to secure the active involvement of individual institutions and firms.**

5.32 At the same time, there may be certain areas in which dialogue could usefully be underpinned by some national research, to provide a framework for more detailed local needs analysis and forestall unnecessary duplication of effort. The needs of small and medium enterprises might lend themselves to this approach, given the very large number of firms involved and the fact that many of their basic needs will be broadly similar. The prior and urgent task of raising basic environmental awareness in the small and medium enterprise sector is already being addressed by the Government through the Advisory Committee on Business and the Environment. **We recommend that the Government should also consider the case for commissioning complementary research into this sector's training needs.**

6 Environmental education for the student body at large

Main points

- FHE has an important part to play in developing the environmental understanding of students whose courses are not specifically 'environmental' in focus.

- Such 'cross-curricular greening' may be concerned with work-related needs, or more broadly with the students' needs as citizens. In practice, much provision may address both sets of needs concurrently.

- Although many employers see a need for 'greening', it has so far received very limited attention within FHE.

- 'Greening' cannot be expected to develop at the same pace, or according to the same set of priorities, in every institution, given the varying circumstances of institutions and the need to deal sensitively with the suspicions which proposals for 'greening' may encounter.

- It is nevertheless high time that each institution adopted a considered strategy, appropriate to its own situation, for the promotion of environmental education across the curriculum.

- Environmental education for 'non-specialist' students may be delivered either through self-contained modules, or by developing environmental themes which arise naturally from the students' main subjects of study.

- In practice a combination of these strategies is likely to be needed, although the range of academic subjects providing scope for the integration of environmental issues is much wider than might be supposed.

- The development of a common level of environmental understanding across the whole of an institution's student body is a difficult objective to achieve in the short term, but experiments towards this end should be encouraged.

- Much more attention should be given by examining, validating, accrediting and professional bodies to the need for more extensive treatment of relevant environmental issues in the FHE curricula which they control or influence. We are particularly concerned that NVQ and GNVQ requirements should encourage, and not impede, the development of 'cross-curricular greening'.

6.1 We now consider FHE's responsibility for developing the environmental understanding of those students – the vast majority – who are not taking specialist courses (as defined in Section 4) or updating courses (as defined in Section 5). For convenience, we refer to the inclusion of environmental issues in 'non-specialist' students' programmes as 'cross-curricular greening'. We do not altogether care for this label, which has unfortunate overtones of 'trendiness'; but as we have previously noted (Introduction, paragraph 8), it is hard to find a concise alternative.

The present situation

6.2 Cross-curricular greening is poorly developed. We wrote to 50 English FE colleges asking, among other things, what action they had taken 'to encourage the study of relevant environmental issues within . . . courses which are not themselves specifically environmental in focus'. Most of the 23 who replied reported some action: but in the great majority of cases this involved a handful of courses for which particular requirements had been imposed, or options made available, by examining or validating bodies. Hardly any respondents had addressed the issue college-wide, although a few intended to do so. This picture is borne out by information from the FEU (paragraph 7.5) and HMI. In HE, the need for greening is perhaps more widely acknowledged in principle, at least by the polytechnics (most of whom have subscribed to a declaration pledging themselves to promote greater awareness of environmental issues through their curricula); but this objective has been pursued far more vigorously by some institutions than by others.

6.3 It is an objective which touches some sensitive nerves, as we have noted in paragraphs 1.9–11: particularly perhaps in HE, with its strong traditions of departmental academic autonomy. Even if the label 'cross-curricular greening' is avoided, the concept provokes mixed reactions. Both in FE and in HE, some institutions, faculties and departments have proved receptive. Others may be resistant to pressures for the adoption of what they may see as an alien agenda, and may also have fears for the coherence and rigour of their courses.

6.4 Such fears cannot be done away with by fiat; and they have some foundation insofar as they reflect a distaste for anything which smacks of 'political correctness'. The head of one HE institution (itself a major provider of specialist environmental courses) wrote to us as follows:

'. . . environmental themes must be used to strengthen the academic rigour of a course. We feel that too often they are introduced as rather trendy makeweights with little intellectually demanding content. Environmental problems and their solutions are extremely complicated. It does environmental education no good if these problems are oversimplified.'

These pitfalls are real. They are likely to be best avoided if the development of 'greening' is carried forward as far as possible by negotiation, and not by imposition.

6.5 But if cross-curricular greening is an objective to be pursued with sensitivity, this detracts in no way whatsoever from the importance of pursuing it. As we have argued in Sections 2–4, specialist courses have an important contribution to make to the development of an environmentally responsible workforce, but their role is likely to remain confined to a fairly narrow front, even in relation to 'practitioners' and 'co-ordinators'. The need for a broader response is even clearer when the workforce as a whole is considered.

6.6 Practitioners and co-ordinators, of course, will often need *post-experience* education or training for their roles; others may need such training to help them see the implications, for their particular jobs, of acting as 'environmentally responsible individuals'. But in either case, initial education can and should be doing much more to lay the foundations of environmental understanding. Nor are we speaking purely for ourselves; among environment-conscious employers, we find much support for what we are saying (as did the Scottish study cited in paragraph 2.5). When we approached major companies at an early stage of our work, roughly half our respondents saw a need for 'greening', at any rate in some subject-areas: the CBI told us that, in their view, 'industry's need is for an environmentally literate workforce, rather than environmental specialists'.

6.7 Beneath the surface of this quotation are two issues which call for comment. We mentioned the first in paragraph 2.1. Although our terms of reference are cast in terms of the needs of the workforce, *This Common Inheritance* stressed the need for an environmentally responsible population, and the role of education in this regard[4]. This wider perspective is not strictly within our remit. Clearly, however, FHE's approach to environmental education will need to take it into account, and we have kept it in mind ourselves because of the very unreal distinctions which we would have had to draw in order to disregard it. Whatever 'environmental literacy' is taken to mean, it must mean much the same for the consumer and the citizen as it means for the worker – at least if it means more than a set of situation-specific 'do's' and 'don'ts' learned by rote and uncomprehendingly observed.

6.8 The second issue concerns the specific role of FHE, bearing in mind the extent to which its students' environmental understanding will have been developed at school. Specific provision is being made through the National Curriculum to ensure that all pupils receive a measure of environmental education as part of their compulsory schooling; and there may be a temptation to assume that once the National Curriculum is fully in place, FHE will have little to add.

6.9 Even setting aside the considerable disappointment felt by some of us about the coverage which has in the event been afforded to environmental education in the National Curriculum, this argument is misconceived on two counts. First – and whatever view is taken of the National Curriculum overall – *individual* students will still be entering FHE with markedly differing levels of environmental understanding, according to their choice of options at Key Stage 4 (age 14–16).

6.10 Second, the need for 'greening' in FHE does not in any case depend solely on the need for basic 'environmental literacy'.

4. Paragraph 17.34: 'Public debate and decisions, including consumer choices, require sound knowledge and awareness of environmental issues. The education system must play an important part in promoting environmental awareness, understanding and competence.'

Whatever foundations have been laid in the schools, there is ample scope – and need – for FHE to build on them. If students are going to enter FHE with greater environmental awareness, they are going to leave it for a world of work in which environmental factors will exercise a steadily increasing influence on policy decisions and working practices. This must create – to put it no higher – a strong presumption in favour of carrying forward what has been achieved at school. Very unfortunate signals will be conveyed if the environment is allowed to disappear from the curriculum at the earliest statutory opportunity, and treated as an 'extra' which students can progressively disregard, the closer they get to the serious business of earning a living.

The way ahead

6.11 For all the importance we attach to 'cross-curricular greening', we recognise that its achievement is not a simple matter. Some general curricular trends within FHE have made it easier. For example, modular course structures provide a useful framework – in terms both of planning and of delivery – for building environmental education into students' learning programmes, whether through modules common to a wide range of courses, or through modules designed (perhaps by adaptation from a 'core' of material) to meet the specific needs of particular groups of students. Some examples of these approaches are mentioned below.

6.12 Nevertheless, 'greening' requires expertise which is very unevenly distributed between institutions. Staff enthusiasm may vary considerably, within institutions as well as between them; and we have already made it clear (paragraph 6.4) that the suspicions which 'greening' will arouse in some quarters cannot sensibly be tackled in a heavy-handed way. It is also necessary to bear in mind the extent to which curricula, particularly though not solely in FE, are nationally determined by examining, validating and professional bodies.

6.13 It would therefore be premature and unrealistic to propose a timetabled master-plan which all FHE institutions should be expected to adopt. For the reasons just mentioned, institutions cannot all be expected to move at the same pace in the short term; and within what is a very broad field, they may quite legitimately differ in their initial priorities. What is important at this stage is a recognition by FHE that the needs described in paragraphs 6.5–7 are real ones – acknowledged by employers as well as environmentalists – which require a serious response. **We therefore recommend that each FHE institution, pursuant to its overall environmental policy (paragraph 7.6), should adopt a strategy for the promotion of environmental education across the curriculum, together with an action plan for its implementation.**

6.14   In Section 7, we shall discuss institutional mechanisms for the development and implementation of such strategies. The rest of the present section looks first at the main curricular approaches which institutions will need to consider (paragraphs 6.15–40), and then (paragraphs 6.41–55) at the external constraints to which we referred in paragraph 6.12.

Alternative approaches to 'greening'

Some general issues

6.15   Environmental education can be delivered in various ways to students taking 'non-environmental' courses. Thus:

a. at one extreme, as we have noted already, there is the self-contained 'environmental studies' or 'environmental issues' module or lecture course, intended for students taking a wide variety of specialist subjects;

b. at the other extreme, the environmental teaching is very closely linked to the students' specialist studies, in the sense that the issues covered are all directly relevant to those studies and are explored and developed throughout their courses as suitable opportunities arise.

6.16   These approaches are not mutually exclusive, and each has possible variations. An obvious variant on a. is the provision of introductory courses which are self-contained, but more closely orientated towards the students' specialisms ('The Farmer and the Environment'; 'Environmental Issues for the Engineer'; etc). In the case of b., consideration may be given to all the main environmental issues which might arise naturally from the specialist subject; or a selective approach may be adopted, whether because of time constraints or for other reasons.

6.17 Which model is appropriate – or practicable – will depend on a number of factors. In particular:

● While most subjects are more 'greenable' than might be apparent at first sight (see paragraphs 6.19-34), the range of environmental issues which can be plausibly 'integrated' in the manner of model b. will vary considerably from one subject to another. (How much this matters depends on whether the institution has set itself the aim of providing a given level of environmental education for *all* its students; this issue is further considered in paragraphs 6.35–40 below.)

● It is possible to 'integrate' a range of environmental issues in a course (in the sense of teaching them in a way which exploits and emphasises their interface with the students' main subjects), without taking any particular steps to elucidate the links between the environmental issues themselves. If the students already know enough to 'make the connections', this may not matter. If they do not, an attempt should be made to bring out these interrelationships and provide the students with a wider framework of environmental knowledge within which to appreciate them.

● Model a. is in principle an effective means of reaching large numbers of students. But the generalised and self-contained teaching of environmental issues, divorced from the students' primary learning objectives, may fail to hold their interest either because of its perceived irrelevance (perhaps the main danger up to now) or because it covers ground with which they are already familiar (which may be an increasing problem in the future).

● These dangers are more readily avoided where environmental issues are integrated as far as possible with students' main subjects: but thoroughgoing integration requires a diffusionof expertise and confidence across the institution which may take a little time to achieve.

In practice, therefore, institutions may need to adopt a combination of approaches, although the aim should be to 'integrate' wherever this is feasible.

Greening in specific subject-areas

6.18 As we have just said, some academic and vocational subjects lend themselves more readily than others to the 'integration' of environmental themes, and we need to explore this point a little further. Without claiming that the borderlines are wholly clearcut, we think that FHE courses can be divided into three broad categories for the purposes of analysis.

Vocational courses

6.19 We have taken this category to include all courses which have been explicitly designed with an eye to the requirements of more or less tightly defined areas of industrial, commercial or professional employment, and also courses in Business or Management Studies (which are seldom specific to particular industrial or commercial sectors, but are nevertheless work-related in a very obvious sense). We are therefore talking about the great majority of qualifying courses in FE, apart from GCSE and A level courses, and also some important areas of HE.

6.20 With courses of this kind, the need – and the scope – for 'integrated greening' seem to us to be exceptionally clear-cut. Any industrial or occupational sector has its potential impact on the environment, and students need to understand what this is and why it matters. We have learned with interest that the following minimum requirement is included in the recommended 'framework curriculum' for the German *Berufsschule*[5]:

5. These establishments provide (in our terms) part-time vocational FE, with fairly broad curricula.

'Trainees should acquire the ability:

● to describe the environmental hazards associated with exercising their occupations and ways to prevent or reduce their environmental impact;

● to describe principles and actions for making efficient use of the energy employed in the context of their industrial occupation.'

6.21   From the information available to us, we are not sure how effectively this recommendation has been implemented in Germany. But at all events we wonder how many students emerging from vocational FHE courses in this country would be able to pass such a test (at the appropriate level of sophistication). There is no doubt that opportunities are being widely missed. For example:

● A recent HMI report[6] observed that, while environmental issues nowadays receive some attention in most agricultural FE courses, 'the material is not always well organised and students do not always appreciate its significance'.

● Despite the increasing part which environmental factors are playing in business decisions, their coverage in business studies courses is still very patchy, even at MBA level.

● Arguing in 1991 against proposals for a reduction in the length of architecture courses, RIBA referred to the need to expand the present curriculum to include (among other things) 'green issues'.

6.22   We have chosen these subject-areas at random, and so far as we can judge they are typical (rather than exceptional) in their treatment of environmental issues. We must also stress that instances of good practice can be found in these subject-areas. Clearly, however, there is a great deal still to be done.

6. *The Response of Agricultural Colleges to Changing Needs*, (Department of Education and Science, 1991).

6.23 As to the ways in which vocational courses can be adapted to give greater attention to the environment, we have learned with particular interest of two developments, one national and one local. Both relate to FE, but in principle the approaches which they embody seem equally applicable to HE. At national level, BTEC is developing a series of modules, intended for optional inclusion in a wide range of National Diploma courses, with the following provisional titles:

Environmental Responsibility
Environmental Science and Technology
Resource Management and Conservation
Environment and Business Practice
Policy and Control
Environmental Investigation.

6.24 The 'Environmental Responsibility' module, for which the content will be specified by BTEC in some detail, will aim to give a broad overview of the contemporary 'environmental agenda', both in scientific and socio-economic terms. This module might be used either in a wholly self-contained way (paragraph 6.15 a. above), or to provide contextual underpinning for the detailed treatment of specific environmental issues elsewhere in the course with which the module is being used (paragraph 6.17, second point).

6.25 For the other five modules, BTEC is not now proposing to prescribe detailed specifications, in view of the wide variety of contexts in which colleges are likely to wish to use them. It is likely that each will be broadly defined, to serve as a framework for college-devised programmes reflecting the particular needs and interests of the groups of students with whom they are to be used.

6.26 There have also been some local initiatives, and we were particularly interested in the curriculum development which has been taking place at one FE college (in the context of an EC-supported Anglo-German exchange project). This has included, among other things:

● the development of two environmental modules for Fashion/Textiles National Diploma students, each covering a range of key environmental issues, for example, energy, waste/recycling, chemicals in the environment, environmental issues and consumerism with specific reference to the textile industry, but with some elements of wider context;

- a similarly-conceived unit for Hotel and Catering students;

- two more broadly-based units intended for inclusion in a relatively wide range of National Diploma courses.

These approaches, as we have already noted, seem potentially applicable to a wide range of vocational education at all levels.

The natural sciences

6.27   The natural sciences, particularly perhaps within HE, cannot be looked at in quite the same way as the 'vocational' subjects. A high proportion of graduates will make extensive use of their scientific knowledge in their subsequent careers, but they will do so in many different industrial, commercial, educational and public service settings; and whereas the content of a truly 'vocational' course will relate to an 'external' reference point (viz., the requirements of a particular type of work), the curricular dynamic of a science course is largely 'internal' to the discipline itself. The traditional single-subject honours degree reflects this emphasis on the mastery of a coherent body of knowledge - an emphasis which tends to result in some suspicion of curricular proposals which are thought to put 'disciplinary integrity' at risk.

6.28   In saying this, we recognise the need for a substantial supply of graduates with a high level of competence in the individual scientific disciplines (including some with the capability to extend the boundaries of knowledge). We also acknowledge the benefits derived by humanity over the centuries through the single-minded pursuit by scientists of their particular disciplines. At the same time, this single-minded approach has dangers where wider contexts are lost sight of. In the particular case of the environment, this implies a need to ensure that students understand three points in particular:

- the distinctive contribution which their discipline already makes to our understanding of the causes and effects of environmental change;

- the limitations of this contribution where it is not complemented and corrected by the insights of other disciplines;

- the main ways in which the application of their discipline is liable to affect the environment favourably or adversely, and the scope for adapting or extending the discipline to enhance its positive contribution.

6.29 There is no single way of achieving this. At the theoretical level, seminars might be arranged to help students appreciate more clearly what the fundamental methodological assumptions of their own disciplines are, and how and why they differ from those of other disciplines (from the social as well as the natural sciences). That approach is, of course, more appropriate to the needs of HE students.

6.30 At the applied level, however, some BTEC Science courses already include environment-related projects, sometimes drawing on case-study material from industry. We should like to see this approach far more widely adopted, in HE as well as FE and the value of such projects will be enhanced if they involve students from different disciplines in a collaborative problem-solving process. There is a useful model, albeit with different objectives, in the joint projects successfully introduced by some institutions for students from the various 'Built Environment' disciplines (Architecture, Surveying, Building, etc). Interdisciplinary projects of this kind require very careful preparation, and space must be found for them within heavily loaded curricula. But we are convinced that their potential value is more than sufficient to justify the effort.

Social sciences, humanities and arts

6.31 The social sciences have their own contributions (in most cases fairly obvious) to make to our understanding of the causes of environmental change, and their own part to play in the search for solutions to particular problems – although on both counts each discipline has limitations similar to those which we have mentioned in the case of the natural sciences. With one or two exceptions, however, the arts and humanities are distanced – at least at first sight – from the environmental agenda (and also, in general, from the world of work, except in the case of those students who go into teaching). There might therefore seem to be little if any scope for 'integrated' treatment of environmental issues on the lines of paragraph 6.15 b. above.

6.32   There is, however, no reason to suppose that students in these subject areas are any less concerned about the environment than their scientific and technological contemporaries: and many of them will go on to occupy positions of responsibility, in industry or elsewhere, in which they are likely to need to come to terms with the 'environmental agenda' in one way or another. On closer inspection of the individual arts and humanities disciplines, moreover, environmental 'connections' do begin to appear. For example:

● man's relationship with - and impact upon - the natural environment can be studied *historically* as well as scientifically;

● *philosophy* can help to elucidate the ethical dimensions of the environmental agenda;

● many *theologians* are taking an increasing interest on the theological implications of the environmental agenda (or, conversely, the environmental implications of their theological assumptions);

● the study of *literature* and *drama* will normally involve consideration of its authors' explicit and implicit values, which may include their responses to nature and the environment. The same can be said of the other creative arts (which can be a very powerful vehicle for the expression of environmental values).

6.33   A 'curricular audit' of an institution's courses may reveal other connections[7]. At the same time, there are dangers in pursuing the 'environmental connections' of humanities subjects indis-

7. See, for example, *Environmental Education for Adaptation* (Centre for Human Ecology, University of Edinburgh, 1991).

criminately. There is little merit in exploring an author's implicit 'environmental values' to an extent which distracts attention from what he or she may be saying, more clearly and significantly, about other important matters. It is also possible for such explorations to drift into a scientifically ill-informed discussion of contemporary environmental issues.

6.34 So while we believe there to be a good case – and legitimate scope – for the 'greening' of humanities courses, we agree also that this is an area in which progress must be made by consent. We note also that, insofar as the 'integration' of environmental issues into such courses is feasible, it is highly unlikely that a *comprehensive* overview of the contemporary environmental agenda can be interwoven in this way. An institution which sets out to offer its humanities students such an overview will therefore normally need to rely, to some extent at least, on the use of the 'self-contained module' (paragraph 6.15 a.) – as one or two HE institutions are already doing through the medium of modular degree schemes offering students a very wide menu of options.

A 'curricular entitlement'?

6.35 In paragraphs 6.15—34 we have sketched out the main ways of providing environmental education for different categories of 'non-specialist' student in FHE. To date, much of the progress made with 'greening' has reflected departmental initiatives rather than institutional strategies; and where it has a strategy, an institution may wish – or be obliged by circumstances – to give priority to particular student groups. However, it is open to an institution to set itself the objective of providing *all* its students with the opportunity to develop their environmental understanding to a given level (or even requiring them to do so).

6.36 This concept of 'curricular entitlement' has begun to appear – though not normally under that name – in HE, where some institutions are aiming to provide all students (or a large proportion of them) with the chance to improve, for example, their foreign language or information technology proficiency. But it is rather more familiar in FE, where there has been a trend in recent years towards greater curricular commonality, with a view to ensuring that adequate attention is given to the needs of all students aged 16–19 in respect of certain basic competences which might otherwise fall between the stools of the specialised curricula which FE has traditionally offered. The Technical and Vocational Education Initiative (TVEI) has been a significant change agent in this area.

6.37 The notion of an environmental 'curriculum entitlement' – at least if this is conceived of in terms of a defined level of understanding and competence to be attained – presents certain problems, both conceptual and practical. It is not too difficult to agree, in broad terms, that the elements of such an entitlement should include some understanding of:

a. the workings of the physical and biological systems which regulate the environment globally and locally, and make it habitable;

b. how, and why, human activity is placing the environment under pressure;

c. the main specific problems, for example, global warming, waste disposal, etc, arising from the pressures at b., and the options available for tackling them;

d. the individual's own responsibility in relation to b. and c.

6.38 Target *levels* of understanding may be harder to define. This is particularly true for FE, given its students' wide ability-range, and the likely need to differentiate between its full-time and part-time students (paragraph 6.48). The situation is further complicated by the arrival of the National Curriculum, the likely impact of which is difficult to predict at this stage[8]. All these factors make for some difficulty in visualising a standard set of targets for 16–19 year-

8. In the sense that many pupils will have had to continue with Science beyond the point at which they might previously have dropped it, the National Curriculum should provide an improved foundation for environmental education in FHE. But the levels of specifically environmental knowledge attained by the age of 16 are likely to vary considerably between pupils (see paragraph 6.9).

olds which are realistically attainable and represent a suitable advance on the baselines from which they will be starting.

6.39 In terms of implementation, the delivery of an 'entitlement' across the whole of an institution is a considerable undertaking logistically, and there is also the question of its 'saleability'. The take-up of 'environmental modules' has been good where institutions have offered them as options which students can take, if they wish, as alternatives to something else. We have less evidence of the typical FE (or HE) student's likely appetite for environmental education where this has to be offered as a net *addition* to his or her programme and taught in a self-contained way. Integration with the students' main subjects can meet these difficulties, but maybe at the cost of restricting the range of issues covered (paragraph 6.17, first point).

6.40 In making these points, our concern is in no way to dissuade institutions from seeking to develop 'environmental curriculum entitlements' (whether under that label or some other). Our point is simply that this is an area in which progress will need to be made empirically and step-by-step, rather than in accordance with any blueprint which we or anybody else might suggest a priori. We therefore hope that as many institutions as possible will feel able to make a start and share their experiences with others. In this connection, we understand that the next phase of the Further Education Unit's project 'Environmental Education Throughout FE' will give some attention to the integration of common environmental learning objectives within otherwise diverse courses. This could shed some very useful light on the issues described above.

The role of examining, etc, bodies

A. Further Education

6.41 One very important factor remains to be dealt with. For convenience of analysis, we have so far set on one side the significant 'external' curricular constraints within which institutions have to work. Even HE is not a wholly free agent in deciding what to teach (see paragraphs 6.51–55); and the great majority of FE courses, at any rate for the 16–19 age-range[9], must meet requirements laid down – with varying degrees of rigidity – by national examining, validating and accrediting bodies. We must now look a little more closely at these influences.

6.42 In FE, there has always been a multitude of 'awarding' bodies, ranging from highly specialised bodies offering qualifications for small numbers of persons in one occupational sector to bodies, like BTEC and City and Guilds of London Institute (CGLI), which are active on a very broad front indeed. This is likely to continue to be the case. But these bodies will themselves be subject to important constraints in future, given the Government's intention to bring all vocational qualifications within the NVQs framework (Annex D). Disregarding those who are catching up on their GCSEs, FE students aged 16–19 will in future fall mainly into three categories:

a. students taking full-time courses leading to NVQs;

b. students taking courses leading to – or counting towards – 'occupational' NVQs (some full-time, but the majority part-time and often supported by Training Credits);

c. students taking A and AS level courses (usually through full-time programmes akin to those offered by sixth forms, although some 16–19 students pursue single A levels by part-time study).

Each type of provision raises distinctive issues.

National Vocational Qualifications

6.43 As we have noted in Annex D, the first GNVQs were introduced in September 1992 in five subject areas, at NVQ Levels 2 and 3. Those at Level 2 comprise six mandatory units which must conform to specifications devised by NCVQ in consultation with other interests. At Level 3 there are eight such mandatory

9. Non-vocational adult education – to use an admittedly unsatisfactory label for an important strand of FHE – falls at best on the fringes of our terms of reference, and we have not in any case had time to consider it in detail.

units, together with four 'optional' units defined by the awarding body (at present usually BTEC, CGLI or Royal Society of Arts).

6.44   GNVQs aim to strike a balance between vocational relevance and broader educational objectives, and might thus be expected to offer a favourable setting for developments of the kind described in paragraphs 6.23–26 above. We have therefore looked with interest at NCVQ's specifications for the five pilot subjects. For Manufacturing, a mandatory environmental unit has been included (*as well as* one on health and safety). Elsewhere, the picture is more patchy. For Business and Leisure/Tourism, some attention must be given to environmental impact, but perhaps in a rather narrow perspective focussed on immediate local impact. In the Art/Design specifications, 'environmental impact' seems to relate essentially to visual impact; and we regret that there is a unit which requires students to assess materials from various standpoints but not, apparently, in terms of their renewability or the disposability of the waste which they generate.

6.45   We recognise that these are early days, and also that there will presumably be scope for strengthening the treatment of environmental issues through the optional units. Nevertheless we see some real risk of missed opportunities. Bearing in mind what we have said above in paragraphs 6.20–21 above, **we therefore recommend that all parties concerned with the future development of GNVQs should ensure that systematic consideration is given in each case to the identification of the main environmental issues affecting the occupational sector in question, and that these issues are included in the specifications in the absence of very strong reasons to the contrary.** In the light of its planned review of other Lead Bodies' standards (see below), COSQUEC should have a part to play in this.

Occupational NVQs

6.46   In relation to occupational NVQs, the situation is more problematical, at least at the lower NVQ levels and on the basis of experience to date. In saying this, we acknowledge that the NVQ system is based on a set of principles which have their own coherence and reflect a real need. Also, as we have noted in Annexes D and E, an NVQ is a qualification based on standards of competence achieved, not a course syllabus. The scope for greening thus depends on two factors: the extent to which environmental competences are included in the occupational standards developed by Lead Bodies as a basis for their NVQs, and the elbow-room available to colleges for 'contextual' teaching which goes beyond what the NVQs themselves specifically require.

6.47   In practice, environmental competences have not so far figured prominently in the specifications for many NVQs. Environmental responsibility does not perhaps lend itself easily to expression in the clear-cut output or 'can do' terms of an NVQ *competence statement*. But there also seems to be quite widespread concern within FE at what is seen as a tendency by Lead Bodies to take a restrictive view of the *underpinning knowledge* to be expected of NVQ candidates – while at the same time leaving colleges little scope for enriching the curriculum on their own initiative (because of the amount of time required for the teaching and assessment of the prescribed occupational skills).

6.48   Two points must be acknowledged in recording these concerns. First, most students pursuing lower-level NVQs are part-time. Any vocational curriculum for such students will be under pressures which will restrict the scope for exploring 'contextual' issues[10], and it would be difficult to claim that the environment has received much attention in most of the craft-level syllabuses which NVQs have been replacing. Second, the scope (or lack of it) for 'cross-curricular greening' is just one aspect of a wider issue about the educational impact of NVQs, which goes well beyond our remit as a Committee.

6.49   The fact remains that, insofar as students seeking 'occupational' NVQs are judged to be in need of further environmental education, we are unclear how readily this need can be addressed within the

10. In view of what has been said above in paragraph 6.20, we should note that most students receiving vocational education and training through the German 'dual system' spend two days a week in college, compared with the one day per week which is normal for part-time FE students in this country.

curricular context which seems to be emerging – unless the NVQ specifications themselves require this. In this connection, we note that COSQUEC's Stage III corporate plan envisages liaison with other Lead Bodies, to encourage the wider and more consistent adoption of integrated environmental competence standards across all relevant occupational areas. This is an important task, and **we urge the Employment Department, in concert with the Department of the Environment, to provide support for COSQUEC to facilitate its speedy completion.**

A levels

6.50 For full-time A level students in FE (and indeed in schools), general or complementary studies programmes are normally provided in addition to their A Level classes. These programmes can clearly be used as a medium for environmental education, albeit on a 'self-contained' basis; and we recommend that all colleges consider whether more use might be made of this opportunity, at any rate until such time as environmental issues feature in a wider range of A Level syllabuses than is the case at present. **This latter issue is one which we would strongly commend to the attention of the School Examinations and Assessment Council and the Examining Boards.**

B. Higher Education

6.51 As a result of the Further and Higher Education Act, most large HE institutions may now award their own degrees without external *academic* validation. But if a degree course aims to prepare students for a specific profession, the institution will wish to ensure that it meets the requirements of the relevant professional body – which may be defined in considerable detail. HE may also provide courses leading to external examinations conducted by the professions themselves, although many professions have been phasing out their own examinations and relying on 'approved' degrees as the educational route to membership.

6.52 We ourselves wrote to a small, selective sample of professional bodies enquiring what action they had taken to promote stronger coverage of environmental issues in the courses which they approve or examine. We have also seen the report of a wider survey carried out as part of the Scottish project referred to in Section 2 above[11]. This involved the despatch of a questionnaire to some 100 professional bodies (mostly covering the United Kingdom, although a few were specifically Scottish). From the 34 responses received, the Scottish researchers concluded that 'most professions provide very little [environmental] coverage [within their qualifications]'; they drew particular attention to the legal and commercial sectors, where none of their seven respondents 'had either an environmental content in their professional qualifications, or an environmental policy'.

6.53 As exceptions, the Scottish study singled out the built environment and, 'to a lesser but significant extent', the engineering professions – the two sectors, in fact, on which we ourselves had concentrated. But even here, the professional bodies have for the most part moved fairly cautiously, and progress has been greatest where (as with Chemical Engineering and Town Planning) the nature of the discipline is such that environmental issues are unavoidable. Most of our own respondents were sympathetic in principle to the case for 'greening', and only one specifically pleaded 'curricular overload'. Where action has been taken, however, this seldom seems to have gone beyond fairly broad exhortation. We also suspect – from the responses to our enquiry, and from what we have been told by HMI and others about the content of current courses – that some (not all) professional institutions and course providers tend to construe 'environmental responsibility' rather narrowly, in terms of purely local damage-limitation and prevention.

6.54 We recognise that professions vary considerably in the nature and extent of their direct environmental impact. It would therefore be unrealistic to expect *every* professional body to insist on the 'greening' of all courses for which it approves (or designs) the syllabus. We also appreciate that some professional bodies have been quite strongly criticised by HE for the excessive rigidity (as HE sees it) of their syllabuses and/or course approval criteria.

11. *Towards Environmental Competence in Scotland: Phase 3: Professional Bodies*, (Scottish Enterprise, 1989).

Calls for 'mandatory greening', therefore, might seem to some of the professional bodies to sit rather oddly alongside the pressures which they face to liberalise their requirements in other respects.

6.55 Nevertheless we are convinced that this issue warrants the attention of an altogether wider range of professional institutions than would seem to have addressed it so far: and also that some of the more environment-conscious institutions could usefully take a more proactive line, at least to the extent of offering firmer and more specific guidance to HE. **We therefore recommend that all professional institutions should seriously assess - or, as the case may be, reassess - the place of environmental issues within those HE courses for which they control or influence the curricula, and take action to promote the appropriate changes.** This reassessment should reflect a forward-looking appraisal of each profession's environmental responsibilities, based on adequate consultation. We trust also that the professional bodies will seek to respond positively where HE institutions themselves put forward proposals for the 'greening' of courses.

7 Local strategies and central support

Main points

- Every FHE institution should adopt and implement:

    a. a comprehensive environmental policy covering all aspects of its environmental performance; and

    b. within that framework, a policy for environmental education.

- Institutions' policies may legitimately differ in their priorities and the management systems devised for their implementation, but they should involve the setting of meaningful and measurable targets and the management systems should be clearly defined.

- While the future development of environmental education in FHE will depend crucially on commitment at institutional level, progress will be substantially facilitated by the provision of national support for the considerable curriculum and staff development effort which will be necessary.

7.1　This Section turns from curricular detail to broader questions of strategy. First we expand upon our references in earlier Sections (especially paragraphs 5.16 and 6.13) to the need for environmental strategies at institutional level. We then consider how the implementation of these local strategies might usefully be supported from the centre.

Institutional environmental strategies : general

7.2　As paragraphs 5.16 and 6.13 have hinted, we firmly believe that an institution's policy on environmental *education* should be developed within the context of a wider strategy – akin to the corporate environmental strategies which a rapidly increasing number of companies are adopting – for improving *all* aspects of its environmental performance. In part, we see this as an objective in its own right. Compared with a chemical plant or a nuclear power station, an FHE institution's environmental impact may be modest. Nevertheless the typical institution, among other things:

- has a multi-million pound turnover;

- has the ownership or use of a good deal of more or less well cared-for real estate;

- is a substantial and more or less wasteful user of energy water, paper and many other materials (by no means all of them 'eco-friendly', and some of them positively hazardous);

- operates a large-scale catering facility which is likely to generate substantial waste;

- is visited every day by large numbers of people, using various modes of transport.

7.3 All this leaves ample scope for good – and bad – environmental practice. *This Common Inheritance* has emphasised the need for a commitment to environmental responsibility across the whole of industry, government and the public services. There is no reason why FHE institutions should feel that this does not apply to them.

7.4 However, the promotion of sound environmental practice in all aspects of an institution's activities – as employer, purchaser, consumer, waste-handler, caterer and property-owner (or developer) – is not simply an end in itself. It is relevant in various ways to the institution's educational mission. In particular:

- if the institution is not seen to be committed to good environmental practice, its attempts to teach students the importance of environmental responsibility will lack credibility

- where an institution adopts an environmental strategy, there is scope (which should be exploited) for involving students – sometimes through course-related project work – in its development, implementation and monitoring

- an institution which takes good care of its site and premises will be more attractive to students and (as many HMI reports have emphasised) provide them with a more satisfactory learning environment

- institutions have increasingly close and frequent contacts with employers. An institution committed to the improvement of its own environmental performance can enhance its credibility with some employers, and may set an example to others.

7.5 FHE has not been wholly unmindful of its environmental performance. Most institutions, for example, have tried to achieve energy savings, if only because of financial constraints. But few have adopted comprehensive strategies. Progress has probably been greatest in the polytechnics (as a result of the Committee of Directors of Polytechnics' 'Greening Polytechnics' initiative), but even there the picture varies. In FE, we ourselves made enquiries of 50 colleges (paragraph 6.2); of the 23 who responded, only a couple had so far adopted formal policy statements, although a further eight had more or less firm plans to do so. An FEU enquiry addressed to *all* FE colleges yielded 90 responses: 47 of the colleges concerned had environmental policies in place or under consideration, but their coverage varied considerably[1].

7.6 There are many important issues currently competing for the attention of senior management in FHE. But the pacemakers have shown what can be achieved, where there is the will. **We therefore recommend that every FHE institution, after consultation with its staff and students, should formally adopt and publicise, by the beginning of the academic year 1994/95, a comprehensive environmental policy statement together with an action plan for its implementation.**

7.7 A typical 'policy statement' will set out the objectives of the policy fairly briefly and broadly, and will need to be supported by detailed documentation dealing with timescales, targets and the attribution of responsibilities for implementation and monitoring.

1. See *Colleges Going Green: A Guide to Environmental Action in Further Education Colleges*, Further Education Unit, 1992, p.11 and Appendix 3.

Institutions must decide which aspects of their environmental performance should receive priority, and what precise mechanisms should be put in place for securing the necessary action. On these matters, helpful guidance may be found in CDP's working documents *Greening Polytechnics* (1990) and *Greening the Curriculum* (1991), and in the FEU publication cited above. We need therefore do no more than stress that a meaningful and effective strategy must embody demanding but realistically-attainable performance targets, and will also need to be:

● widely publicised within the institution, so as to enlist the commitment of its staff and students;

● comprehensive in its coverage of the issues mentioned above in paragraph 7.2 (see the publications just cited, for ways in which these issues may affect the way an institution conducts its day-to-day business);

● based on an initial appraisal of the institution's environmental impact, which should be followed by regular 'audits' to assess progress towards existing targets and provide a basis for setting future targets;

● supported by a management system which is properly integrated with the institution's overall systems of governance and management.

7.8 **We further recommend that the Further and Higher Education Funding Councils should take appropriate action to encourage and reward the adoption of sound environmental practice in the institutions which they fund.** Such action might include, for example:

● ensuring that careful consideration is given to the likely environmental impact of capital projects for which earmarked funding is sought ;

● ensuring that financial savings achieved through improved environmental performance accrue to the benefit of the institutions which have achieved them;

- requiring institutions to include particulars of their environmental policies in their overall strategic plans;

- encouraging the adoption of meaningful environmental Performance Indicators across their respective sectors.

7.9 The new planning and funding arrangements for FHE are still taking shape, and we have not attempted to work out these suggestions in detail. But we commend them to the serious attention of the Councils. The public funding disbursed by the English and Welsh Councils will amount to several billion pounds a year, and there is ample scope for them to take a legitimate interest in the environmental responsibility with which this money is spent, at a time when the Government is rightly concerned to improve the environmental performance of the public sector as a whole.

Institutional strategies for environmental education

7.10 **Within the framework of its overall environmental policy, and on the same timescale, each institution should establish a policy for environmental education, likewise on the basis of consultation with staff and students.** In saying that the one policy should be set within the framework of the other, we recognise that many of the key roles in the development and implementation of the two policies will fall to different sets of people. To some extent, therefore, separate planning and management systems may be needed for the two policies, although it is important to secure overall co-ordination at the appropriate level within the institution's general management structures.

7.11 Institutions with policies on environmental education have set about their development in different ways – some of which are illustrated in the CDP and FEU publications mentioned above – and there is clearly much scope for detailed variation. But there are certain broad principles which seem to us to be generally valid.

Scope of the policy

7.12 We would expect most institutions' environmental education policies to be mainly concerned with the promotion of cross-curricular greening. But if an institution is involved, or is contemplating an involvement, in the provision of specialist qualifying courses or environment-related updating, this should be brought within the overall framework of the policy – on a basis, however, which respects the proper responsibilities of specialist departments and course teams for the planning of individual courses, and which likewise seeks to work with, and not against, the institution's existing arrangements (if any) for the co-ordination and promotion of updating provision generally.

Auditing (initial)

7.13 Particularly in relation to cross-curricular greening, we would stress the importance of carrying out an initial institution-wide 'audit' to establish:

a. the extent to which the institution's courses are already giving attention to environmental issues;

b. the availability of relevant expertise among the institution's staff.

The results of such audits, where they have been carried out, have sometimes revealed unsuspected sources of strength, on which institutions have been able to build. Such initial auditing seems essential in any case to provide a basis for setting rational and realistic priorities, and a baseline for measuring subsequent progress.

Targets and priorities

7.14 Some policy statements which we have seen have included very ambitious objectives, particularly in the area of cross-curricular greening. Useful though such long-term aspirations are as a backdrop, worthwhile progress will in practice depend on the adoption of clear short-term targets which are regularly reviewed, and progressively added to, in the light of systematically monitored progress. For reasons already explained in paragraphs 6.4 and 6.12, the targets should be negotiated rather than imposed. They are likely to vary from institution to institution, in terms of the range of courses affected and the curricular modifications to be achieved, and initially they may need to be quite modest. For most institutions, whatever their longer-term objectives, the need at this stage is to capitalise on such expertise and enthusiasm as exists – wherever in the institution it exists – to make a meaningful and measurable start.

Co-ordination

7.15   The arrangements so far made by institutions for developing their environmental education strategies and monitoring their implementation have varied, but have typically involved:

a. the establishment of a co-ordinating Committee (which may or may not also have responsibility for the institution's overall environmental strategy);

b. the designation of one or more staff – existing or specially-appointed – with responsibility for the development and promotion of the strategy institution-wide, and sometimes also the designation of individuals to be responsible for promoting the strategy within their faculties or departments (and for representing their faculties/departments in discussions at institutional level).

7.16   These are very early days to judge the relative merits of the detailed organisational systems which institutions are adopting. In any case the effectiveness of any strategy will depend above all on the commitment of the senior management of the institution, however this is expressed 'constitutionally'. We would however emphasise the importance of ensuring:

● that the functions and authority of the Committee at a. and the staff at b. are clearly defined, within the wider context of the institution's academic planning and quality management systems;

● that staff given special responsibilities in connection with the strategy have adequate time to devote to those responsibilities;

- that the involvement of senior management should go hand in hand with a 'consultative ethos' involving students as well as staff, and designed to create a sense of 'ownership' in the strategy across the institution.

Success will depend on whether these conditions are met, rather than how.

Support from the centre

7.17 The commitment of individual FHE institutions, formally embodied in strategies for environmental education, is, we believe, a necessary condition of any substantial progress in this field; and we believe also that initiatives at the level of the individual institution can achieve a good deal (as some institutions have already shown). The *pace* at which progress can be made, however, is dependent on other important factors.

7.18 The paths we have sketched out in Sections 4–6 of this Report imply a need for substantial curriculum and staff development. In the case of specialist environmental course provision, institutions will presumably identify any such needs and arrange for them to be met within the ordinary course of business (as they do – or should – when developing specialist courses in any subject). Cross-curricular greening, however, will require large numbers of staff to enlarge the scope of their teaching to accommodate issues with which they are unfamiliar, and on which the available expertise within their institutions may be limited. There may be some similar common needs in the area of updating, although – as we have indicated in paragraph 5.28 – much staff development in this field will need to be relatively informal and often related closely to the needs of specific clients.

7.19 Organised staff development covers, in principle, a wide range of activities, from one-off events to programmes of an altogether more extended kind. At the latter end of the spectrum – and from the other side of the Atlantic – we have learned of a very ambitious (and, we gather, successful) staff development programme run by the Tufts Environmental Literacy Institute (TELI) at Tufts University, Massachusetts, to promote and support cross-curricular greening. The centrepiece of TELI's programme is an annual two-week seminar, usually attended by about 40 staff from Tufts and elsewhere. The seminar deals in some depth with a range of key environmental issues which participants, on return to their own Departments, then seek to incorporate in their own teaching programmes, with ongoing support from TELI staff.

7.20   Transplanting this model may be something of a pipe-dream in view of the resource implications[2], but the 'cascade' method employed by TELI could no doubt be replicated on a smaller scale. However, our main concern at this stage is not with the funding of staff development activities at the local level. **Insofar as the future funding arrangements for FHE involve earmarked provision for staff development in particular subject-areas, we would urge the Funding Councils to give serious consideration to the claims of environmental education.** That said, the resources devoted overall by FHE to staff development are substantial. Given the necessary commitment on the part of an institution – without which little progress is likely to be made anyway – it is reasonable to assume that some provision can and will be made within its staff development budget for environmental education, whether or not any special support is provided from the centre.

7.21   The larger problem – particularly in relation to cross-curricular greening – concerns the availability of suitable resources in the form of guidance for teachers and materials for use in the classroom. To some extent, teachers seeking to introduce environmental issues into their courses may be able to produce their own materials, and to some extent they probably should. But an extensive reliance on in-house material would involve formidable duplication of effort up and down the country, and the quality of such materials will in any case depend crucially on the level of environmental expertise available to the individual institution.

2. We gather that the costs of the Tufts seminar are met in full by a private sponsor

7.22　It is therefore important, in our view, to ensure the availability of a sufficient range of high-quality materials nationally. In part, this may be a matter of identifying materials which already exist and bringing them to the attention of teachers whose normal professional reading does not include the relevant environmental literature. It is also fair to assume that, where a high level of clearly-defined demand can be guaranteed, (for example, through the inclusion of substantial environmental components in a widely used national syllabus), some suitable material will be produced commercially on the initiative of individual authors and publishers. We believe, however, that a more co-ordinated initiative is needed.

7.23　Here, a welcome start is being made by the Council for Environmental Education's 'Education and Training for Industry and the Environment' project (which was foreshadowed in paragraph 17.50 of *This Common Inheritance* and is being supported from the Department of the Environment's Environmental Grants Fund). As part of this project, an attempt is being made to identify good cross-scurricular greening practice in the following subject-areas:

- Engineering

- The Rural Environment

- The Built Environment

- Science and Technology

- Business and Management

- Tourism, Catering and Leisure

- Health and Social Services

- Humanities and Social Sciences

- Art, Design and Performing Arts.

7.24 Work in each subject-area has been assigned to a different HE institution, and is being led by staff from that subject-area – an important and commendable feature, given the concerns which we have ourselves expressed in Section 6 about 'imposed greening'. Each institution will host a seminar, involving employers as well as educationalists, in the spring or early summer of 1993 to present its findings. It is hoped that this will then lead to the publication, for each subject area, of a booklet giving guidance on (and some illustrative examples of) good practice. The guidance will be aimed at HE, but may also have some relevance for FE.

7.25 Although this is a valuable initiative, its scale is modest and we have little doubt that one of its main outcomes will be to highlight the need for an altogether more extensive development programme involving further work, by a co-ordinated multi-disciplinary team appointed on secondment or short-term contract, on:

- the identification and documentation of good practice;

- the establishment of a database summarising existing available materials;

- the development of further materials (probably including both 'trainer training' materials and materials for classroom use), following suitable research and consultations both with education and with industry to establish needs;

- the organisation of staff development activities to disseminate the materials.

7.26 As to the organisation and commissioning of such a programme, we suggest that a contract for its delivery might be awarded to a suitable FHE institution (or consortium of FHE institutions) selected after competitive tendering against a more fully worked-out specification. **We recommend that resources be made available to support a development programme along these lines.** We would add that, whoever is responsible for the central co-ordination of the programme, the range of potential participants in its work extends beyond the formal FHE system to include, for example, voluntary organisations concerned with the environment. A number of voluntary sector projects recently funded by the Department of the Environment's Environmental Grants Fund and Environmental Action Fund have produced materials which could with benefit be more widely used as teaching resources.

7.27　We have one other recommendation, which is concerned with encouragement rather than support. When NUS gave evidence to us they suggested, among other things, the institution of a national scheme for awarding a 'kitemark' ('Green Flag' was their suggested title) to any FHE institution whose environmental practices and performance were judged to comply with a set of agreed criteria. We have reservations about the feasibility of a scheme of quite this kind; moreover the British Standard for Environmental Management Systems (BS 7750) provides an alternative national kitemark (albeit in respect of non-curricular environmental performance) for which some FHE institutions may in due course wish to apply.

7.28　At the same time, we see great attractions in the idea of a competitive annual awards scheme to recognise outstanding (as distinct from satisfactory) achievement by individual institutions, whether in terms of the development and implementation of their environmental education strategies or in terms of their general environmental management. 'Environmental' competitions for FHE (sometimes one-off) have been organised in recent years by a number of industrial and other sponsors; such initiatives have provided a valuable stimulus, and we would not wish to see them disappear. But they could usefully be complemented – not necessarily at great cost – by a more 'official' scheme, endorsed by Government but drawing also on sponsorship from industry, commerce and major environmental bodies. **We recommend that the feasibility of establishing such a scheme should be investigated by the Department for Education, the Welsh Office and the Department of the Environment.**

8 Conclusion

8.1 We were asked to recommend priorities for the development of environmental education in FHE. In responding to this remit, we have suspended judgment on a number of issues. We have not, for example, tried to define target levels of environmental competence which FHE should aim to develop in all its students, or looked in depth at the conceptual and organisational issues involved in promoting a fully 'interdisciplinary' approach to environmental teaching in FHE. In sketching out the lines on which 'cross-curricular greening' should develop, we have not sought to specify precisely how far and how fast the process should be carried.

8.2 These are significant issues. But they must also, we believe, be seen as issues for the longer term; and while the discussion of long-term goals has its place in education (as in any sphere of activity), it can very easily distract attention from the need for action here and now. In the field of environmental education there is much that FHE can and should be doing, without waiting for a consensus on longer-term targets to emerge. Arguments about the 'greenability' of English Literature courses provide no justification for deferring action on Engineering and Business Studies. Whatever the likely future trends in demand for specialist environmental qualifications, we believe that some existing specialist courses should be looking carefully at their objectives. And if the market will ultimately determine the boundaries of FHE's role, we are in no doubt that FHE should be making every effort to extend its involvement in environment-related updating.

8.3 Some FHE institutions have made significant moves on some of these fronts. But over much of the system – as we have stressed more than once in this Report – the overriding need at this stage is to make a serious start. This must involve the setting of meaningful targets. But we firmly believe that progress will be most effectively and fruitfully achieved if these targets reflect priorities which each institution has debated and determined for itself in the light of this Report. Solid initial achievements, even on a fairly limited front, will provide the soundest basis for the progressive development of an institutional strategy. Experience gained in this way will also shed much-needed light on the longer-term issues mentioned in paragraph 8.1.

8.4   What is required at present, then, is a pragmatic approach. Pragmatism, however, must be combined with urgency: and just as each institution should rigorously monitor the progress of its own environmental education strategy, we think it essential that the development of environmental education within FHE should be adequately monitored at national level. At some stage, also, the time will be ripe for a closer look at the longer-term issues. **Accordingly, we conclude by recommending that the Department for Education and the Welsh Office should commission, not later than the academic year 1995/96, a national appraisal of the progress which FHE has made in the development of environmental education against the background of this Report: and should consider the need for further action at national level in the light of this appraisal.**

Annex A
Terms of reference

In the light of the available evidence on the levels and main forms of environmental knowledge, skills and awareness which the workforce will need in order to respond to the current and anticipated requirements of the economy and society for greater environmental responsibility:

a. to assess the main strengths and weaknesses of current environmental provision (excluding research) in FHE in England and Wales, taking account of the treatment of environmental issues within the generality of scientific, technological and vocational course curricula as well as the provision of courses which are principally concerned with specific aspects of environmental management or with environmental issues more generally; and

b. to recommend priorities for the future development of environmental FHE (as defined in a. above), with particular reference to:

   i. the respective roles of initial education and vocational continuing education and training concerned with the updating of knowledge and skills;

   ii. the relative priority to be accorded to the different strands of provision identified in a. above;

   iii. the most effective and practicable means of strengthening the treatment of environmental issues (where relevant) within vocational courses which are not themselves specifically environmental in focus;

   iv. the role of interdisciplinary courses in Environmental Science or Environmental Studies.

The recommendations at b. should be directed, as appropriate, to FHE institutions, examining and validating bodies, professional institutions, and other bodies with significant influence on the content of curricula within FHE.

Annex B: Membership of the Committee and sub-groups

The Committee

Chairman

Professor Peter Toyne, Vice-Chancellor, Liverpool John Moores University

Members

John Bunnell,	Managing Director, Retail Division, British Polythene Industries PLC
Professor David Chiddick,	Executive Pro Vice-Chancellor, De Montfort University
Charles Duff,	Corporate Development Manager, Norsk Hydro (UK) Ltd
Peter Fearns,	Principal, Burton-on-Trent Technical College
John Ferguson,	Director, London Waste Regulation Authority
Dr Cecil French,	Engineering Consultant to and Director of Ricardo International PLC
Professor Kenneth Goulding,	Academic Director and Deputy Vice-Chancellor, Middlesex University: previously (to 31 December 1991) Dean of the Faculty of Science, Lancashire Polytechnic
Professor Kenneth Gregory,	Warden, Goldsmiths' College, University of London: previously (to 30 September 1992) Professor of Geography and Deputy Vice-Chancellor, University of Southampton

Professor Dennis Hawkes,	Department of Mechanical and Manufacturing Engineering, University of Glamorgan
Ann Limb,	Director, Milton Keynes College
Dr Anil Markandya,	Department of Economics, University College London (withdrew from the Committee at the end of September 1992 on appointment to a post at Harvard University)
Brian Morris,	Environmental Consultant, John Laing PLC
Professor Timothy O'Riordan,	Professor of Environmental Sciences, University of East Anglia
Dr John Potter,	Principal, Farnborough College of Technology; Editor, *The Environmentalist*
Dr Barry Prater,	Manager of Environmental Services, British Steel (Technical), Rotherham
Dr Sally Richardson,	Senior Education Officer (Tertiary), World Wide Fund for Nature
Giles Sturdy JP,	Council Member, National Farmers' Union
Keith Turner,	Executive Co-ordinator, Council for Occupational Standards and Qualifications in Environmental Conservation
Professor Chris Wilson,	Professor of Earth Sciences and Chair, Environmental Education and Training Group, The Open University

Assessors

John Bushnell,	Department for Education[1]
Stephen Crowne,	Department for Education
Dr Joe MacConnell,	on behalf of the Secretary of State for Scotland's Working Group on Environmental Education
Dr Stephen Martin,	HM Inspector
Brian Whitaker,	Department of the Environment

Secretariat

Peter Fulford-Jones,	Department for Education
Tom Jenkin,	Department for Education (to February 1992)
Kate Hedger,	Department for Education (from April 1992)
Peter Akinwunmi,	Department for Education (to August 1992)
Malcolm Harris,	Department for Education (from August 1992)

1. John Bushnell also acted as Secretary to the Committee's sub-group on Updating, assisted by Ray Foggo and Jeannette Alderson (Department for Education).

Sub-groups

Sub-group on the Needs of Industry and Other Employers

Chairman: Charles Duff

John Bunnell
John Ferguson
Dr Cecil French
Professor Dennis Hawkes
Brian Morris
Dr Barry Prater
Keith Turner
Professor Chris Wilson

Andrew Blaza (CBI) attended the sub-group's first meeting by invitation.

The sub-group met twice.

Sub-group on Developments within Further and Higher Education

Chairman: Professor Kenneth Goulding

Peter Fearns
Professor Kenneth Gregory
Ann Limb
Dr John Potter
Dr Sally Richardson
Giles Sturdy

By invitation, Dr Ted Neild (Committee of Vice-Chancellors and Principals) attended the sub-group's second meeting, and Ms Shirley Ali Khan attended its third.

The sub-group met three times.

Sub-group on Cross-Curricular Greening

Chairman: Peter Fearns

  Professor Kenneth Goulding
  Ann Limb
  Brian Morris
  Dr John Potter
  Keith Turner
  Professor Chris Wilson

The sub-group met twice.

Sub-group on Specialist Environmental Course Provision

Chairman: Professor Kenneth Gregory

  John Ferguson
  Dr Cecil French
  Professor Dennis Hawkes
  Dr Barry Prater
  Dr John Potter
  Dr Anil Markandya

Professor Keith Bardon, Dr Paul Birch and Dr David Chambers
(Committee of Heads of Environmental Sciences) attended the
sub-group's first meeting by invitation.

The sub-group met twice.

Sub-group on Updating and Staff Development

Chairman: Charles Duff

  John Bunnell
  Professor David Chiddick
  Dr Cecil French
  Dr John Potter
  Dr Sally Richardson

The sub-group met twice.

Annex C: Parties assisting the Committee with information and advice

Organisations giving oral evidence to the Committee

The following organisations took part in the special meeting referred to in paragraph 3 of the Introduction to the main report:

Confederation of British Industry (Nicky Chambers)
Business in the Environment (Patrick Mallon)
Institution of Environmental Sciences (John Bull)
National Union of Students (Richard Hermer, Doug Taylor and Nigel Jackson)
Council for Environmental Education (Dr Ewan McLeish, Shirley Ali Khan, Ken Thomas, Tony Thomas, Stella Vesey)

Organisations represented at sub-group meetings are shown in Annex B above.

Other organisations providing information and/or advice

Employers, employer associations and trade associations

Industrial and Commercial
Albright & Wilson Ltd
Amerada Hess Ltd
APV PLC
Aspinwall & Company
BAA PLC
Bowater PLC
BP International Ltd
British Aerospace Ltd
British Airways
British Chemical Engineering Contractors' Association
British Coal Corporation
British Effluent and Water Association
British Gas

British Nuclear Fuels PLC
British Polythene Industries PLC
British Steel
Chemical Industries Association
Courtaulds PLC
Dragon International Consulting Ltd
Engineering Industries Association
Esso UK PLC
Exxon Chemical Ltd
Ford Motor Company Ltd
Foster Wheeler Energy Ltd
Hinton & Higgs (Consultants) Ltd
Hydro Fertilizers Ltd
ICI Group Headquarters
Intercity
J Henry Schroder Wagg & Co Ltd
J Sainsbury PLC
John Mowlem & Company PLC
Johnson Matthey
Johnson Wax Ltd
Kingfisher PLC
KPMG Management Consulting
Legal & General Group PLC
The Marley Roof Tile Co Ltd
Monsanto PLC
National Association of Waste Disposal Contractors
National Power
National Westminster Bank PLC
North West Water Group PLC
Phillips Petroleum Company
Pilkington PLC
Richard Costain Ltd
Rolls Royce PLC
Safeway PLC
Shell UK Ltd
ShellMex
Simon Engineering PLC
Slough Estates PLC
Staveley Industries PLC
Tarmac Industrial Products Ltd
Tesco PLC
Thames Water PLC
TI Group PLC

TSB Group PLC
Welsh Water PLC
Wolstenholme Rink
WRc

Conservation bodies, public authorities, ete
Association of County Councils
The British Trust for Conservation Volunteers
Groundwork Foundation
Her Majesty's Inspectorate of Pollution
National Rivers Authority
National Turfgrass Council
Nature Conservancy Council for England
The Royal Society for the Protection of Birds
The Wildfowl and Wetlands Trust

Further and Higher Education Institutions[2]
Accrington and Rossendale College
Anglia Polytechnic
Aston University
Basford Hall College
University of Bath
Berkshire College of Agriculture
Beverley College of Further Education
Bishop Burton College of Agriculture
Blackpool and Fylde College
University of Bradford
Brighton Polytechnic
Bristol Polytechnic
Brockenhurst College
Brunel University
Buckinghamshire College of Higher Education
Burton upon Trent Technical College
Capel Manor Horticultural and Environmental Centre
Charles Keene College of Further Education
Chester College of Higher Education
Chichester College of Technology
Clarendon College
Cricklade Tertiary College
Croydon College
Derbyshire College of Higher Education

2. Institutional names are those current at the time the information was
provided to the Committee

Dudley College of Technology
Dunstable College of Further Education
University of Durham
University of East Anglia
East Warwickshire College
Exeter College of Art and Design
University of Exeter
Fareham Tertiary College
Farnborough College of Technology
Hall Green College
Harper Adams Agricultural College
Hatfield Polytechnic
Hopwood Hall College
The Huddersfield Polytechnic
University of Kent at Canterbury
Kingston Polytechnic
Lancashire Polytechnic
University of Lancaster
Langley College of Further Education
Leeds Polytechnic
University of Leeds
Leicester Polytechnic
Imperial College, University of London
King's College, University of London
School of Oriental and African Studies, University of London
University College, University of London
Longlands College of Further Education
Loughborough University of Technology
Manchester Polytechnic
University of Manchester Institute of Science and Technology
Mid Kent College of Higher and Further Education
Middlesex Polytechnic
Milton Keynes College
Nene College
Newcastle College of Further Education
Newcastle upon Tyne Polytechnic
University of Newcastle upon Tyne
North East Surrey College of Technology
North Lindsey College
North Nottinghamshire College of Further Education
Northbrook College of Design & Technology
Northampton College
Open University

Oxford Polytechnic
Peterlee College
Plymouth College of Further Education
Preston College
Reading College of Technology
Richmond upon Thames College
Roehampton Institute
Salford College of Further Education
Sandwell College of Further and Higher Education
Sheffield City Polytechnic
University of Sheffield
Soundwell College
South Bank Polytechnic
The South Downs College of Further Education
South Kent College of Technology
South Nottinghamshire College of Further Education
South Thames College
Polytechnic South West
University of Southampton
Stradbroke College
Strathclyde Graduate Business School
St Helens Community College
Sunderland Polytechnic
University of Surrey
University College of Ripon and York St John
University College of North Wales
Thames Polytechnic
Walsall College of Technology
Polytechnic of Wales
University of Wales College of Cardiff
West Nottinghamshire College of Further Education
The Polytechnic, Wolverhampton
Worcester College of Technology
Writtle College
University of York

Survey of taught postgraduate courses (report, paragraph 4.31)

Completed questionnaires were received in respect of the
following courses:

Brunel University, MSc in Environmental Pollution Science
  University of Durham, MSc/PG Dip in Ecology

University of East Anglia, MSc in Atmospheric Sciences

Kingston Polytechnic, MSc in Earth Science and Environment

University of Leicester, MSc/PG Dip in Natural Resources Management

Birkbeck College, The University of London, MSc in Environmental and Analytical Chemistry

Birkbeck College, The University of London, PG Dip (extra-mural) in Ecology and Conservation

Imperial College of Science Technology and Medicine, University of London, MSc/PG Dip in Environmental Technology

Imperial College of Science Technology and Medicine, University of London, MSc/PG Dip in Environmental Engineering

University College, University of London, MSc/PG Dip in Conservation

University College, University of London, MSc in Environmental Design/Engineering

University of Manchester Institute of Science and Technology, MSc in Integrated Pollution Management

University of Manchester Institute of Science and Technology, MSc/DipTechSci in Pollution and Environmental Control

University of Newcastle upon Tyne, MSc/PG Dip in Environmental Assessment and ManagementOxford Polytechnic, MSc/PG Dip in Environmental Assessment and Management

Portsmouth Polytechnic, MSc in Applied Toxicology

Portsmouth Polytechnic, MSc in Biodeterioration of Materials

Portsmouth Polytechnic, MSc in Environmental Change

The University of Reading, MSc/PG Dip in Renewable Energy and the Environment

The University of Reading, MSc/PG Dip in Wildlife Management and Control

The University of Sheffield, MEng/MSc Tech in Combustion Science and Pollution Control

The University of Sheffield, MSc/PG Dip in Process Safety and Loss Prevention

University of Salford, MSc/PG Dip in Environmental Resources

University of Surrey, MSc/PG Dip in Applied Industrial Technology (modular)

University of Surrey, MSc/PG Dip in Radiation and Environmental Protection

University College of North Wales, Bangor, MSc in Ecology

University College of North Wales, Bangor, MSc in Environmental Forestry

University College of North Wales, Bangor, MSc in Marine Environmental Protection

University College of North Wales, Bangor, PG Dip in Rural
  Resource Management
University College of Wales, Aberystwyth, MSc/PG Dip in
  Environmental Impact Assessment

Professional institutions

British Institute of Management
The Chartered Institute of Building
The Chartered Institution of Building Services Engineers
The Engineering Council
Institute of Biology
Institute of Ecology and Environmental Management
The Institute of Physics
Institute of Wastes Management
Institution of Chemical Engineers
The Institution of Civil Engineers
The Institution of Electrical Engineers
The Institution of Environmental Health Officers
The Institution of Environmental Sciences
The Institution of Structural Engineers
The Institution of Water and Environmental Management
The Landscape Institute
The Royal Institution of Chartered Surveyors
The Royal Society of Chemistry
The Royal Town Planning Institute

Other organisations and individuals

Agricultural and Food Research Council
Agricultural Training Board
Business & Technology Education Council
City and Guilds of London Institute
Committee of Heads of Environmental Sciences
Committee of Vice-Chancellors and Principals of the Universities
  of the United Kingdom
Council for Occupational Standards and Qualifications in
  Environmental Conservation
Economic and Social Research Council
The Environment Council
Mr Peter Howard

Institute of Directors
Natural Environment Research Council
North Nottinghamshire Training and Enterprise Council
Professor J K Page
Polytechnics Central Admissions System
Science and Engineering Research Council
The Universities Central Council on Admissions
Waste Management Industry Training Advisory Board

Annex D: National Vocational Qualifications: background note

1. Although their implications for HE are as yet unclear, National Vocational Qualifications (NVQs) have already made a major impact on FE in England and Wales[1]. It is Government policy that all vocational FE for full-time students aged 16—18 should be brought within the NVQ framework. This Annex provides a brief outline of the NVQ system, for the assistance of readers not already familiar with it. When fully in place, the system will comprise two types of qualification: NVQs which are based on national standards of 'occupational competence', and general NVQs (GNVQs) which are more broadly based.

NVQs

2. Compared with a traditional vocational qualification, an NVQ provides an altogether clearer attestation that its holder possesses the specific 'competences' needed to function effectively at a given level in a given occupation. The main features of the system are as follows:

   ● each NVQ is based on competence standards defined by a 'Lead Body' drawn mainly from employers and employees in the relevant industry or occupational sector;

   ● the standards are expressed in terms of outputs: that is to say, in terms of what the candidate must show that he/she can do. Attainment of these standards will require a foundation of 'underpinning knowledge and understanding', but the acquisition of this knowledge and understanding is treated as a means to an end and not an end in itself;

   ● candidates will normally be assessed in the workplace (or, if this is impracticable, under conditions which simulate those of the workplace as closely as possible);

   ● anyone who believes that he/she can demonstrate the necessary competences (or possesses evidence of having attained the requisite standards of competence) may apply to be assessed, whether the competences have been acquired through FHE, through on-the-job training or simply through workplace experience.

1. The NVQ system described in this Annex also covers Northern Ireland. In Scotland, there is a parallel system of Scottish Vocational Qualifications (SVQs).

3. While most Lead Bodies do not, at present, specifically include standards of environmental competence within their NVQs, certain Lead Bodies are wholly or quite substantially concerned with aspects of environmental management. These include, for example, COSQUEC, the Waste Management Industry Training Advisory Board (WAMITAB), and the Board for Education and Training in the Water Industry (BETWI).

GNVQs

4. GNVQs will offer young people aged 16–19, and adults who wish to take them, a middle way between A levels on the one hand, and occupational NVQs on the other. They are intended to provide both a broad preparation for employment and a sound basis for progression whether to HE or to job-specific NVQs. The first GNVQs were introduced in September 1992 in five vocational subject areas (art & design, business, leisure and tourism, health and social care and manufacturing).

The NVQ levels

5. All NVQs are allocated to one of five standard levels. The table below sets out these levels and indicates their 'equivalences'. (It should be stressed that these equivalences are broad: for example, the traditional usage of such terms as 'Advanced Craft' and 'Higher Technician' is by no means consistent across industrial sectors.)

NVQ Level	Description	Broadly equivalent to
5	Professional Management	Higher Education
4	Higher Technician, Junior Management	Higher Education
3	Technician, Advanced Craft, Supervisor	2+ A Levels (or equivalent in AS Levels)
2	Basic Craft	4+ GCSEs grades A–C
1	Foundation	Other GCSEs

Annex E: Practitioners, co-ordinators and specialist qualifications

1. This Annex looks more closely at the available evidence of labour market demand for persons holding 'specialist environmental qualifications' as defined in paragraph 4.1 of our report. As we have emphasised in paragraph 4.6, expressed employer demand (or the lack of it) has never been, and should never be, the sole determinant of what the FHE system sets out to provide. That said, assumptions about environment-related employment opportunities are pretty clearly influencing institutions' decisions to provide environment-related courses and students' decisions to enrol for them. Questions about employer demand cannot therefore be dismissed as irrelevant.

2. Where a specific demand exists for persons with specialist environmental qualifications, it is reasonable to assume that this will very largely reflect demand for competent environmental practitioners and co-ordinators. A growing need for such persons can be expected over the next few years, and beyond. Even if industry sets out to do no more than comply with the law, this will entail a significant investment of managerial, scientific and technical man-hours. Legislation will also have implications for the enforcement agencies, as well as providing work for the expanding environmental consultancy sector. Employment in voluntary and public sector conservation bodies is also likely to expand (although it is harder to say how rapidly). These prospective needs were acknowledged by the great majority of the employers we consulted.

Current employer preferences

3. However, environmental work is not, in general, highly professionalised at present – if we take 'professionalisation' (*not* the same as professional*ism*) to denote a situation in which a function is reserved for holders of closely tailored qualifications acquired through extended study (at whatever level). In Environmental Health and Town and Country Planning this does apply, but neither the EHO nor the Planning Officer is a typical

'environmental practitioner. Closer to our central concerns (as defined in paragraph[1] of the Introduction to our report) are Water and Waste Management, each of which has a professional body (the Institution of Water and Environmental Management and the Institute of Wastes Management). Membership of both institutions, however, is open to anyone who meets certain industrial experience requirements and holds appropriate qualifications in a relevant subject (usually engineering or natural science), and the specialist Diplomas offered by both institutions are taken by very few people.

4. A similar preference for more-or-less-broadly relevant (as distinct from highly job-specific) qualifications is widespread across all the employment sectors mentioned in paragraph 2 above. The following paragraphs summarise the results of the soundings which we have taken of employers.

Industry and commerce

5. The viewpoint of most of the employers we consulted can be summarised along the following lines:

a. *environmental co-ordinators* in industry will have reached their present positions via a wide variety of career paths, and will usually have other management responsibilities not directly related to the environment;

b. many of the competences required by industrial practitioners and co-ordinators will be very similar to those required by other scientific, technical and managerial staff;

c. the scientific and technical competences at b. will usually need to be acquired by studying a traditional scientific or technological subject, such as, engineering or chemistry - to the appropriate level (usually first degree or maybe BTEC Higher National). The further knowledge and skills required in order

1. On the work of Environmental Health Officers, see paragraph 4.10 of the main report. Planning Officers are of course very much concerned with environmental issues as defined in paragraph 6 of our Introduction: but the Planning profession originated long before the contemporary 'environmental agenda' took shape, and many of the concerns with which Planners deal are substantially independent of that Agenda

to apply these competences to the solution of environmental problems (which may be industry- or even company-specific) are best developed by post-experience education or training.

6.   Most industrial and commercial employers therefore see, at most, a modest role for persons with specifically-environmental qualifications, at least at first degree level and below. Some industries have special requirements: for example, there is demand from the food industries for persons qualified in Environmental Health. But the general view is sceptical; Environmental Science graduates, for example, are widely thought to lack the depth of scientific knowledge which real-life environmental problem-solving requires in an industrial setting.

The conservation sector

7.   Full-time conservation staff are likely to need a blend of knowledge and skills – many of them practical and inter-personal – which cannot be acquired simply through a course. Where conservation bodies expect staff to hold relevant academic qualifications, they usually interpret 'relevant' fairly broadly. This by no means disqualifies (say) graduates in Environmental Science or Environmental Management; but they can usually expect to face strong competition from holders of single-subject qualifications.

Regulatory bodies

8.   Recruitment at professional level to HM Inspectorate of Pollution is restricted to persons with prior industrial or other relevant experience (who will mainly be qualified in relevant traditional scientific and technological disciplines)[2]. The National Rivers Authority is prepared to consider persons with specifically environmental qualifications (such as Environmental Science degrees) for a significant proportion of its graduate-level posts – but alongside holders of single-subject degrees in relevant

2. The postgraduate course mentioned in paragraph 4.42 of the report is an integral part of the training programme provided for HM Inspectors (and also attracts significant numbers of students from elsewhere).

disciplines such as Chemistry, Biology or Geology (depending on the nature of the post).

Environmental consultancies

9. Organisations describing themselves as environmental consultancies vary considerably in their size (from self-employed individuals to firms with over 100 staff), in the range of services which they offer and in the clienteles which they serve. It is therefore difficult to generalise about the recruitment preferences of this amorphous sector (or to estimate the size of the sector with any reliability). Openings for holders of specialist qualifications clearly exist in parts of the sector. But where a consultancy serves a largely industrial clientele, its recruitment policies may well resemble those of its clients.

Possible future trends

10. At present, then, most employers are doubtful whether FHE should be seeking to meet the needs of practitioners and co-ordinators through specialised courses of *initial* education (even if they can be identified as discrete target-groups at this stage, which they often cannot be). To a considerable extent, we think they are right. Two points, however, must be made on the other side.

11. First, employers' attitudes will reflect what they know about the specialist courses and qualifications available hitherto. Many employers may have an incomplete picture of the current range of courses; and where their criticisms have substance, some of them might be met by some reorientation of existing courses. This possibility is discussed in paragraphs 4.21–30 of the main report, in relation to Environmental Science and Environmental Studies graduates. We must however stress that, while the measures we have advocated should make these graduates more widely *acceptable* in the labour market, it does not necessarily follow that employers will develop a widespread positive *preference* for them.

12. Second, in speaking of practitioners and co-ordinators we are talking – particularly though not only in the case of industry –

about occupational roles which are in many cases new, or at any rate fairly newly *identified*. As clearer definitions of these occupational roles evolve, further scope for specialist courses may become apparent. This assumption seems to underlie the first degree courses discussed in paragraph 4.12 of the main report (Environmental Management, Technology, etc), and also many of the postgraduate courses discussed in paragraphs 4.31–44. As noted in the main report, there is as yet very little evidence on which to judge the effectiveness with which the undergraduate courses have been targetted; such information as we have been able to gather on the postgraduate courses is reasonably encouraging.

Occupational standards and NVQs

13. Some of the courses mentioned in paragraph 12 have been introduced in response to more or less sharply-focussed requests from employers. Essentially, however, they represent ad hoc initiatives by individual institutions. Nationally, clarification of occupational roles (and their educational requirements) will result from the development of Occupational Standards and NVQs especially by the Lead Bodies mentioned in paragraph 3 of Annex D. We note in particular that:

a. WAMITAB's first NVQs (Levels 3 and 4) will be closely linked to – possibly identical with – the certificates of technical competence which waste-operators will require under the *Environmental Protection Act* 1990. Since there have up to now been *no* recognised waste management qualifications at this level, the arrival of these NVQs will give rise to new training needs.

b. The first stage of COSQUEC's work has involved the development of NVQs, at Levels 2–4, for a wide range of occupations in the environmental conservation sector. These will be available from early 1993. In the next phase of its work, COSQUEC aims to develop standards and NVQs (initially at Level 4) in Environmental Resource Management (and Building Conservation) which should be relevant to a wide range of practitioners and co-ordinators, including those in industry.

14. In considering the implications for FHE, however, it is important to bear in mind the sharp distinction which the NVQ system draws between *qualifications* and *courses*. As noted in Annex D, it is possible in principle to obtain an NVQ without *any* formal off-the-job education or training, although in some cases this may be difficult in practice. So far as can be judged at this stage, environmental NVQs are likely to fall into three categories:

a. NVQs affording little or no scope for FHE, either because very little off-the-job instruction is required, or because this can be readily provided in other ways. For example, many of the training needs generated by BETWI's NVQs are likely to be met through the water industry's well-established in-house training arrangements.

b. NVQs for which FHE can provide a fairly comprehensive - and cost-effective - preparation through courses which are similar to traditional vocational courses in length and mode of attendance (although their content may need to be rather different, particularly in terms of the balance between theory and practice). Some of COSQUEC's Environmental Conser-vation NVQs are likely to fall into this category.

c. NVQs for which FHE's role will be confined to teaching the 'underpinning knowledge and understanding' (or aspects of this), leaving the specific vocational competences to be developed in other ways. WAMITAB's first NVQs may be of this kind, as may COSQUEC's Environmental Management NVQs (since many candidates will be starting from a baseline of considerable prior experience). To seize these opportunities in face of possible competition from others, FHE will need to offer programmes which are flexible in delivery while being closely tailored in content.

15. It will also be noted that the environmental NVQs so far developed (or under active consideration) have been at Levels 4 and below. Insofar as they generate new educational requirements, therefore, these will be largely at FE or sub-degree HE level. In certain areas, professional-level (Level 5) environmental NVQs are likely to follow, but the timescale is uncertain and it is difficult to predict at this stage just how far it will be either feasible or desirable to modify existing provision to take account of them. The dovetailing

of degree course curricula with NVQ requirements is a particularly complex issue, on which work has barely begun (in any subject-area).

Printed in the United Kingdom for HMSO
Dd295626 1/93 C25 531/3 12521